Preparing
the Way

The Reopening of the John G. Lake
HEALING ROOMS in Spokane, Washington

by
Cal Pierce

Preparing
the Way

The Reopening of the John G. Lake
HEALING ROOMS in Spokane, Washington

by
Cal Pierce

"As the well of God's healing presence has been re-dug, a strategic door has been opened that will impact the move of God's Spirit around the world. It will become an unpolluted stream of signs and wonders glorifying the Lord Jesus Christ!"

Jim W. Goll
Ministry to the Nations
Franklin, Tennessee
Author, The Lost Art of Intercession

"The reopening of the Healing Rooms of Spokane, Washington, has helped to pave the way for what should become the greatest healing revival of all history. This book is a must-read!"

Bill Johnson, Senior Pastor
Bethel Church
Redding, California

"As a person who has been miraculously healed, I believe the love and the vision of the Healing Rooms is essential to God's purposes today. It must be embraced by America and the world if we are to see the expression of the true nature of the Kingdom of God in the earth."

Mickey Robinson
Seagate Ministries
Franklin, Tennessee

"The John G. Lake Healing Rooms are one of the clearest testimonies of how prophetic intercession is re-digging the ancient wells of revival. What Cal Pierce has seen is an explosive encouragement for every person claiming the covenantal inheritance of the past."

Lou Engle, Associate Pastor
Harvest Rock Church
Pasadena, California
of Re-digging the Wells of Revival

D0002841

DEDICATION

To our son, David, who is with the Lord. He inspired us to pursue God with a passion and hunger that can change our world.

CONTENTS

FOREWORD

I first met Cal Pierce several years ago when Pastor Bill Johnson and myself were asked to minister at a conference for the dedication of the Healing Rooms in Spokane. I heard at that time the stories recorded in this book. It was exciting to hear of how God was obviously leading Cal to reopen the Healing Rooms of John Lake, and it was no less exciting to be able to read the story in this wonderful book. I believe God is using Cal Pierce to sound a wake-up call to the Church in North America to be responsive to Jesus' mandate in the Great Commission. This mandate clearly includes a ministry of healing on the part of the Church. Surely Matthew 28:18-20 looks back to and includes Matthew 10:7-8.

Just a few days before I read this manuscript, I had Cal in my local church, the Vineyard Christian Fellowship in St. Louis. I must confess that parts of his teaching were "stretching" for my wife and myself, but we believed it was a good stretching. We, too, had become too passive in regards to the ministry of healing. Considering that healing is probably my strongest emphasis in ministry, it is significant to say that Cal challenged me.

Although I thought of some pastoral concerns that could arise out of his teaching (especially if it was misapplied), I did not try to compromise what he was saying. I believed his insights were biblical, I appreciated his teaching on persevering in prayer until the manifestation of your healing appears, and I agreed that the Bible teaches healing as part of the atonement.

I find it very interesting that almost all of the men and women who have been powerfully used in the healing ministry through the years have held this viewpoint. I long ago discovered that my reasons for rejecting this viewpoint formerly were based on experience, not on the Scriptures. It was while reading F.F. Bosworth's book *Christ the Healer* that I realized that my position was not biblical, and from that time until now, I have held the position that healing is indeed in the atonement. Now, Cal Pierce has helped me to see some other remaining inconsistencies in the practice of my theology.

While Cal and his team were in my church, two of our women, Kim and Laurie, received powerful healings from fibromyalgia, from which they both had been suffering for many years. They had been prayed for many times in the past, but had not been healed.

Both of the women had been severely limited in what they could do, and suffered the chronic pain common to those who have this disease. Laurie could not even be in our worship service because the sound waves caused her such severe pain that it would take her two days to recover.

This past Sunday they both stood and testified of their healings, and our people rejoiced with them. Laurie goes to a chiropractor to whom others in our congregation also go. He was very excited about the changes in her body and told her to keep getting more prayer because it was obviously working.

Cal Pierce is a dedicated Christian — humble, sincere, well-read, nonpompous, loving and full of faith. God once again has chosen the weak and foolish by this world's standards to confound the strong and the wise. He has chosen another "Little ole me" through whom He will receive the glory. Thank you, Cal, for the important work you are contributing to the Church in North America, and thank you for the wonderful faith-building testimonies in this book.

I want to caution every reader. This book will challenge your view regarding healing, your practice in the ministry of healing, and especially any skepticism you have harbored regarding this ministry that was so much a part of Jesus' work on earth, of the ministry of His disciples and also of their disciples. Healing was a vital part of the early postapostolic Church ministry, and it is an important part of the ministry of the Lord Jesus Christ through His Church in the twenty-first century.

I highly recommend this *Preparing the Way* to all those who are interested in building their faith for healing.

Randy Clark, Senior Pastor
Vineyard Christian Fellowship
Founder, Global Awakening
St. Louis, Missouri

INTRODUCTION

John G. Lake, a Canadian by birth, was sent by God to Spokane, Washington, about 1914. It was not his first assignment. He had served as a missionary to South Africa with great success. Now he had a burden for the sick of America and an assurance that God would give him a healing ministry here in this country.

John Lake was led to put together a team of men and women whom he came to call "healing technicians" and to open a suite of rooms in downtown Spokane where those men and women of faith could minister to the sick. What happened in those rooms in the Rookery Building was so amazing that they came to be called the Healing Rooms.

Within five years of the opening of the Healing Rooms, there were a hundred thousand documented healings. As a result, a representative of the Federal government in Washington, D.C., declared Spokane to be "the healthiest city in the world." Officials at the only hospital in Spokane at the time, Deaconess Hospital, didn't care much for John G. Lake and his ministry. The miracles God was doing in the Healing Rooms were causing them to run out of patients.

There was a clear healthcare choice in Spokane. If a person was sick, he could go to the Deaconess Hospital to be medicated or cut on, and then he would receive a large bill for these services — even though they may or may not have helped. The alternative (which most people came to prefer) was to go to the Healing Rooms in the Rookery Building and be prayed for by the "healing technicians." The usual result was that the patient was healed, and there was no charge for the service.

When God sent my wife and me to Spokane eighty years after the original Healing Rooms had closed, we were sure that He had not changed. He is still saving the lost, and He is also still healing the sick. We had begun to experience His healing power ourselves in a wonderful revival in our hometown of Redding, California, so we knew that His power was just the same as it had been in the time of John G. Lake. Indeed, it was just the same as it had been in the time of the apostles.

But healing was clearly not flowing in Spokane as it had in those former days. As we prayed and sought God to know why, He showed us that the wells of healing had been stopped up with doubt, unbelief and the traditions of men. We needed to re-dig those wells that had brought so many miracles to the sick of Spokane in a previous time. The story of how this was accomplished, how the Healing Rooms were reopened at the very same address as before, and how God began to do the same miracles of healing as in that former time is one that has challenged people all across the country in recent years. Many men and women, upon seeing or hearing about the success of the Healing Rooms in Spokane, have been moved to open Healing Rooms in their own cities, and such ministries are quickly being established across this country and in a number of other countries as well.

Here, for the first time in print, is the story of how it happened in Spokane, and how it can happen in your town. May you, too, be blessed and challenged as you read *Preparing the Way*.

Cal Pierce
The Healing Rooms
Spokane, Washington

And heal the sick that are therein, and say unto them, The kingdom of God is come nigh unto you. Luke 10:9, KJV

ONE

THE CURTAIN GOES UP

Andy Butcher of *Charisma* magazine did a wonderful job of describing the opening of the Healing Rooms. Let us begin the story with his words as the curtain rises:

CHARISMA NEWS SERVICE
Monday, November 06, 2000   Vol. 2 No. 174
LEAD STORY:

Historic Healing Ministry Reopened After Eighty Years in Spokane, Washington

Pioneer John G. Lake's historic Healing Rooms praying for the sick once again

A pioneering healing ministry has been resurrected after a break of almost eighty years. Reports of physical and emotional healings are piling up at the Healing Rooms in Spokane, Washington, which have opened at the same address used by famous early 1900s healing evangelist John G. Lake. The Healing Rooms are manned by prayer volunteers from local churches, under the direction of former real estate developer Cal Pierce, who says God led him to "re-dig the wells" of Lake's ministry. Pierce believes that a new move of healing is due to sweep the country, to prepare Christians for a major harvest: "If we are going to be an army marching to battle, it won't be on crutches."

Since the Healing Rooms restarted almost eighteen months ago, more than five thousand people have visited for prayer. Some have traveled from overseas, as word of the ministry has spread. Local doctors have referred patients to the ministry. Volunteers have sent out hundreds of prayer cloths. Healing Room ministries have also been started or are planned in around a dozen other cities.

"The key here is we are not trained up as great counselors, or as a great deliverance ministry, but we are trained up to receive the presence of the Holy Spirit to come and do the work," Pierce says. "And when He comes, every bit of infirmity must go. The key is humility and unity, to receive the presence of the Holy Spirit to come and do what He wants to do."

Shaken by a touch from God at his former church in California in 1996, Pierce felt led to move to Spokane and later gave up his business interests for full-time ministry. He regularly visited Lake's grave site to pray — "it had to do with the Holy

Spirit and the power that man walked in that I knew was still available for the Body of Christ." Then he believed he should reopen the Healing Rooms.

Pierce was amazed to find space on the third floor of the downtown Rookery Building, at the same location Lake had ministered from 1914 to 1920. A former missionary to Africa, Lake's ministry was so successful that, at one stage, Spokane was reportedly called "the healthiest city in America." He dreamed of a string of similar healing centers across the country, starting one in Portland, Oregon, but he died of a stroke in 1935.

Steve Goodenberger of Spokane still weeps when he talks about the impact of the new Healing Rooms on his family. The Presbyterian music minister's teenage son Keith's schooling had been crippled by years of migraine headaches, with no professionals able to help. They decided to try the Healing Rooms, and after a couple of visits the pain disappeared. "He has been a new creature ever since," his father says. "It has changed our lives."

Before he went to the Healing Rooms, Todd Callaghan, of Coeur d'Alene, Idaho, had been told by doctors that his days were numbered by a rare genetic condition. But since receiving prayer, he says that his pain has lessened significantly and that several cancerous tumors have disappeared or shrunk. "It has changed my life completely. I don't know if I would still be here without it."

Currently open four days a week, the Healing Rooms have eight separate rooms where teams of three receive visitors and pray for them. Reports of healings are pinned to the wall. "We will continue with people as long as it takes," Pierce says. "We have had a lot of people healed 'as they went.' "

by Andy Butcher

— Two —

The Genesis of the Burden: David's Heart

Many people ask me how I happened to receive a burden for the reopening of the Healing Rooms in the first place, and I have to admit that it didn't begin in my own heart. It actually came from the heart of David, our youngest son.

When David was just seven years old, he was diagnosed with Duchenne type (pseudohypertrophic) muscular dystrophy, a disease whose common symptom is the weakening and wasting away of healthy muscle tissue. Duchenne affects children, and those who have it typically do not survive to become adults. By the time David was ten, he was already confined to a wheelchair, and he needed our help to do most things.

Michelle and I divided the labor in this regard. For instance, it was her job to get David up in the morning and get him ready for school, and it was my job to put him to bed every night. He had a motorized wheelchair and was able to get around at school and to wheel himself around the house. During the night, we would take turns getting up to turn him over every two hours so that he would not develop bedsores. By the time he was sixteen, David could move only his hands and his head.

As his physical condition deteriorated, however, David began to develop a heart after God. This was interesting, because my wife and I were stuck in a sort of religious mode at the time. We were Christians, but we were not very excited about the Lord and were not really praying like we should have been. We went to church on Sunday mornings and took David with us, but we were not interested in other services. Suddenly, David wanted to be in every service. He didn't want to miss the Sunday evening service or the youth service. I would load him up in the van and drop him off at church, and then I would go somewhere to have coffee, do some shopping or just walk around until he was finished. Then I would pick him up, and we would go home.

David's passion for God increased to the point that he would call me to his room each evening to help him get ready to read his Bible. I had built a special table for him that he could wheel his chair under. When he was ready, I would help him get his arms and hands up onto the table and then put the Bible where he could manipulate the pages of it. He would sit there and study the Bible for the next several hours.

After David had read the Bible for two hours or more each evening, then he would begin to pray. We always left his door open so that we could hear him if he needed anything, and occasionally throughout the evening, when I would pass by on my way from the television to the bathroom, I would hear him praying. He was actually interceding for others. He was praying for America, for his classmates, for our neighbors and for us, his parents and siblings. David had a heart for people who were hurting, and he felt their needs.

When I would hear him praying like this, my heart would break. Why didn't I know God the way my son did? He had such a passion for the things of the Lord. Why didn't I share that passion? We had often given him opportunity to do other things, but this was what he wanted to do. In fact, this was *all* he wanted to do. Knowing God better was his sole desire. He wasn't interested in other things. He wasn't even interested in his sickness. It did not consume him, as is the case with many sick people. He was consumed with his desire for God.

Occasionally, as I was heading to work late in the morning, I would see David and his classmates in the school yard as I drove by. Most of the children were playing on the courts, but David was always sitting over by the gymnasium alone in his wheelchair. The thought of my son not being able to be involved in the activities of the other children was one that devastated me personally. From David's perspective, however, this wasn't bad at all. Being alone and apart from the rest of the group, he could talk to the Lord. I had a hard time understanding his way of thinking, but I was deeply convicted by his deep devotion to God.

We had a large deck that wrapped around the house, and David was able to maneuver his chair out there into the fresh air when the weather permitted. We would hear him out there, going back and forth, talking to God.

One evening my wife and I heard David crying and rushed to his side. He had wheeled himself into the hallway. "What's wrong?" we asked. He said that he had had a bad thought, and it was easy to see that this had broken his heart. That deeply sincere confession crushed me. I had many bad thoughts, but I had grown so calloused that I never let that fact bother me. David loved Jesus so much that having one bad thought had brought him to tears. Again, I felt ashamed of myself.

One day we asked David, "If you could have any wish, what would you ask for?" I was sure he would say that he wanted to get up and walk like other kids and do the things they were doing. That would have been very normal for any boy David's age. He didn't answer quickly. His eyes moved up to the ceiling, and he looked there for a few minutes, obviously searching his soul for the answer. When he finally answered, it surprised both of us: "Nothing!" he said.

I couldn't believe what I was hearing. My son, who was practically helpless and had very little to look forward to in life, did not feel the need for anything at all. How could that be? I thought about all the things I wanted for myself, and the things for which I might have asked, given the same opportunity, and they were many. But David was sufficiently filled by his knowledge of and his love for Jesus so that he didn't need anything else. How utterly amazing!

Throughout his seventh and eighth grades and on into high school, every paper David wrote for class was about Jesus. Jesus was his life, and everything he did was about the Lord.

Then, for a period in 1989, each evening, when I would go into David's room to get him ready for bed, he would ask me if he could stay up a little later because he had more that he wanted to pray about. Even though he had school the next day, each evening he wanted to extend this time even more. "Can I please stay up just a little later," he would plead. I think he would have prayed all night, if I had let him, but around 11:30 I would go in and insist that he just had to get some sleep so he could go to school the next day. David reluctantly agreed.

When I finally did start getting David ready for bed each of those nights, I would find that his clothes were wet from perspiration because of his exertions in prayer, so wet that they stuck to his body. Even his socks and shoes were wet.

After this had gone on for about ten days, I asked David one night what was so important that he was exerting himself so in prayer. His answer amazed me. "We've been studying Russia in class, and I'm praying that the walls of Communism will come down so that the Gospel can go into that country and the people can be saved."

My God, I thought, *how could such a young man have a burden like this?* I had never prayed for the Iron Curtain to fall, and yet my sixteen-year-old son was doing it, and with such fervency. What motivated him?

Not more than thirty days after that happened, the lead story on all the news programs was that the Berlin Wall had been breached, and I saw the East German people pouring through it and tearing it apart piece by piece. I was overcome with emotion and began to weep. If the prayers of a teenager could have such an effect, surely God would hear me too. If David's prayers could shake a nation and tear down a wall, then I must begin to do my share.

Suddenly I desperately wanted to know God as David did. I cried out to God, "God, I want to know You, and I will know You in the way David does." The change I sought as a result of David's impact on my life did not come immediately, but it would come.

A few years later, before his twenty-first birthday, David slipped away from us and went to be with his Savior. One moment he was here, and the next he was gone. In one sense, Michelle and I were devastated. We had loved him so much. But in another sense, our cup was full. We felt very privileged to have had David in our home. He had left us with a vision, a vision to work toward the saving of America, a vision to bring healing to our nation and our people. In time, that vision would become clear.

THREE

OUR SPIRITUAL ROOTS

The shame of our spiritual lethargy during those years was that we should have known better.

Michelle and I both grew up in Redding, California. She was raised Catholic, and I was raised Baptist. After we married, I went to church with her. I quickly learned when to stand, when to sit and when to kneel. I desperately wanted to blend in so that it would not be obvious how very out of place I was.

Going to church an hour or so each week didn't bother me — as long as it didn't interfere with my life. I was in the process of developing my business as a building contractor and real estate developer, and that took a great part of my attention. My work provided adequately for our lifestyle at the moment, and we lived comfortably with our three children. Needless to say, neither Michelle nor I was born again. We knew who God was, but we didn't know Him personally.

One day some of our neighbors told Michelle about a special prayer meeting to be held in the basement of the Catholic church. They called it a "Charismatic" gathering and said that the meeting would be led by a layperson, a psychiatrist. I couldn't imagine what that would be like, so I agreed to go.

The meeting was very unlike what I had come to expect in church. For one thing, everyone joined in songs of worship. I could recognize some of the songs from my days as a Baptist. That day, for some reason, these songs moved me, and I was soon fighting back tears. Before the service had ended, Michelle and I had both accepted Jesus as our Lord and Savior right there in the basement of that Catholic church.

We loved the folks who attended the Charismatic prayer meetings, and we enjoyed having fellowship with them. Quite a few of them were also involved with a group called the Full Gospel Business Men's Fellowship International (FGBMFI). This group, made up of ministers and laypeople alike from many different denominations, had regular meetings in Redding, and we also began to attend their meetings. During these meetings, many wonderful testimonies were shared by people of a variety of denominations whose lives were being changed through a genuine relationship with Christ.

It was through attending those meetings that we met people who were attending Bethel Assembly of God church in Redding, and in time, Michelle and I began to visit that church and take our children to Sunday school there. After Sunday school, we would then go on to our Catholic service. Little by little, we began going to Bethel more and to our own church less, until we eventually made Bethel our church home. By the mid-seventies, things were looking up in our spiritual lives.

In time, I became an elder and board member at Bethel and chapter president of the FGBMFI in Redding. I was also involved in many FGBMFI regional activities. As I said at the beginning of the chapter, we should have known better, but a time of spiritual drought was approaching, as we, like so many others before us, began to lose our first love.

— Four —

Stagnation

After we had been members of Bethel Church for many years, I began to fall into a pattern of spiritual stagnation. Several things contributed to this spiritual decline. For one thing, the real estate market had slowed seriously in California, and having invested in a number of office buildings, we were suddenly losing ground fast financially. This concerned us and took extra time to try to remedy. The uncertainty of the future sometimes left us feeling emotionally drained.

Another contributing factor was our circle of friends. We had become involved with a group of people from the church who owned recreational vehicles (RV's), and they sometimes took us along when they went out "RV'ing." We enjoyed these activities a lot, and it seemed that we had so much in common with the group that we all went out together every Friday night for dinner and later to take in a movie. We looked forward to these occasions, and they became very important to us. I personally enjoyed "RV'ing" so much that I had made my plans for our retirement years. We would sell the business, buy ourselves a nice RV, and just travel enjoying America.

And those years were not very far away. I could feel them approaching, and I was looking forward to them. I was tired of struggling with business, and worst of all, I was tired of the church.

This was terrible, because I had been a board member and an elder of the church for twenty-five years already. I now say that I must have been the most bored board member the church ever had. Things had gotten so bad in my spiritual life that I didn't even care if we went to church or not. I was only there on Sundays because I had to be. Otherwise, I wouldn't have been there.

On some Sunday nights, Michelle would say to me, "Don't you think we should be at church? After all, you're on the board." But I always had a good excuse for not going. I had to get ready for work on Monday, and I needed my rest — or whatever else I could think of at the moment. I had fallen into a form of Christianity that denied the power of it, and I was unconcerned about changing my spiritual status ... until David's passion began to stir my heart.

Other members of the church could not have known how bad things were with my soul. I carried my Bible like a good Christian; I said all the right things; and I dressed the right way; but I was living in a dry and thirsty land, just waiting for my opportunity to get away from it all.

Until then, I did what I considered was required of me in the church, but nothing more. I was always in church on Sunday mornings, and I attended the occasional board meetings, but I thought that was more than enough.

Life went on like this for far too many years, and even though I had felt convicted of my lifestyle through seeing David's passion for Christ, I didn't really know what to do about it.

— FIVE —

REVIVAL!

In January of 1996, we elected a new pastor at Bethel, Reverend Bill Johnson. At first, I thought Bill might be my last choice.

As part of the committee that would select a new pastor for the church, I was aware that we were to interview three candidates, and when I knew that Bill was one of them, I was not enthusiastic. I knew Bill and had known him for many years. His father had been the pastor at Bethel when our family first began attending the church many years before.

And I liked Bill. Even when he was young, he had developed a youth ministry downtown called The Salt House, and I had actually been involved in it off and on. Now, however, I felt that we needed new blood, someone from the outside, someone from another city, someone we had not known before. I was sure that when the moment came, I would vote for one of the other two candidates.

As it happened, I was unable to be in the meetings at which the three men were interviewed, but I later listened to the tapes of those interviews. As I did, I heard something in Bill Johnson's voice that moved me. It so moved me, in fact, that I changed my mind and supported him to be our next senior pastor.

We were not aware of it at the time, but Bill had been crying out to God for about twelve years for revival in Redding and for a new wave of healing to come. God was hearing his prayers. Not long after he came to town, some very unusual things began to happen.

One Friday night, one of the RV couples told us about some unusual things that were happening in the meetings that Bill and one of the Vineyard pastors were conducting in some area churches. People were falling down, laughing, shaking and crying. On the way home, Michelle asked me what I thought and if we should go see for ourselves. I said to her, "Those are meetings that we are *not* going to." I didn't like the sound of anything that would upset my plans for the future. I liked the program I had outlined in my mind, and I didn't want anything to change it.

In May of that year, Bill called for a special meeting for all the leadership of the church. By then the membership of the church had grown to two thousand, and with the school, there were many of us involved in the activities of the church. He sensed that not all was well with the staff he inherited, and he was believing for revival for us. God knew that I needed it.

I wasn't happy when Michelle read the letter of

"invitation" to me on the way home from church one Sunday morning, but she pointed out that the pastor was requiring everyone in leadership to be there. So I went.

With the board members, the office staff, the school staff, the Sunday school teachers and the youth leaders, there were about a hundred of us who met one evening in the new room behind the sanctuary. The church people were calling it the Great Room, but because of what happened there, I have come to call it the Upper Room.

The meeting opened with prayer, and someone led us in a series of worship choruses. Then, suddenly, Bill was standing before us. He had his hands upraised to Heaven, and he was saying, "Come, Holy Spirit!" The next thing I remember is that wave after wave of fire began to course through my body. The flames seemed to be going deep into my bones, and that made me want to run or jump or shout or scream or all of those things at once. But I couldn't move. My feet were stuck to the floor, as if they had been glued there.

Within what seemed like a few minutes, I heard Michelle's voice. She was pulling on my sleeve, trying to get my attention. "Honey," she was saying, "the meeting's over, and everyone's gone home." I had no idea what the meeting had been about, but I somehow knew that I would never be the same again.

I tried to move again, but couldn't. It took two strong men to pull me loose from the floor that night, and from then on the change in my life was so great that it was like the difference between night and day.

For many years, I had been content to sit and let the world go by — just so it didn't bother my regular routine. Now I couldn't sit still for the life of me. I had to be doing something for God all the time. I simply had to be in church every time the door was open. If there was a prayer meeting being held before the evening service, I had to get there for the prayer meeting. And, even then, I always went early, sometimes an hour early, because I didn't want to miss anything.

I prayed for an hour before each prayer meeting to get ready for the prayer meeting, I prayed to get ready for the evening service, and I loved to go to the altar in every service and pray some more. What's more, I was loving every minute of it. If I could have moved my bed into the church and stayed right there praying, I probably would have. I had become such a fanatic that my friends began to worry about me, and my social life began to suffer.

I couldn't explain it. Somehow Cal Pierce had died in that Upper Room, and I was now somebody else, somebody very different. When Cal Pierce died, all of his plans and desires died with him. None of those things interested me anymore. I wanted God's program for my life, and I resisted anything that would interfere with that.

There was no desire in me to attend the Friday night dinner and movies I had loved so much, and going RV'ing seemed like the most boring thing we could possibly do. Several people complained to Michelle, "Cal's become so heavenly minded that he's no earthly good." When she would tell me what they said, I didn't know what to answer. "I don't know what's happened to me either. All I know is that I want more of God. There is nothing I will not do to touch Him the way I long to." I just kept pressing in.

The closer I got to God, the more this caused a problem with my friends. This amazed me. After all, what was church for if not to get closer to God? Could they not be happy for me that I had left my spiritual lethargy and gained a new zeal?

Anyway, I couldn't be bothered with what they thought. My purpose in life was now to serve God, to spread His Gospel and to see lost souls saved. What others did was their business. I was beginning to really live.

Six

Getting Started
in the Healing Ministry

Suddenly, I had an inexhaustible desire to study everything I could get my hands on about spiritual growth. I was particularly interested in revival, and I read every book I could find on revival and revivalists.

I also read everything I could find regarding healing and men and women who were used in the healing ministry. For instance, I read many books about the great Smith Wigglesworth. I also read all I could find about Maria Woodworth-Etter, John G. Lake, Alexander Dowie, Charles Parham, Jack Coe, A.A. Allen, Kathryn Kuhlman and many others. I went through more books in the space of a year and a half than I had read in my entire life — four years of college included. I just had to have more, and I couldn't get enough.

I began to press in to the revival that had come to Bethel Assembly. Ministry teams were being formed to minister salvation to the lost, the Holy Spirit to those who were hungry and healing to those who were sick. I would not have missed that opportunity for the world.

In each service, our teams gathered at the front to minister to those who had come forward for prayer. So many came forward, three or four hundred at a time, that we had to move eight or ten of the front rows of chairs out of the way to make room for this ministry. When we had finished praying, most of the people would be on the floor under the power of God.

What a joyful time this was for us! We felt like we were in Heaven. There was a wonderful spirit of unity among the members of the ministry team. This was not church as usual; this was church on fire.

As I studied the lives of the great men and women who had been used in healing, I became convinced that God hadn't changed and that we could expect the same results today. Soon I began praying for the sick myself.

The first two people I prayed for to be healed were both gravely ill in the hospital, and both of them subsequently died. I often use this as an illustration to encourage those who are just beginning to pray for the sick. We all have to start somewhere, and we all have a lot to learn about healing the sick.

The fact that the first two people I prayed for died didn't discourage me. This only increased my determination to press in and receive the healing power that others had exhibited in the past. I was convinced that Christ was still the Healer, and that He still wanted to heal men and women who were suffering. My failure was not His fault.

I remember well the first healing miracle that happened as a result of my prayers. Gary and Jane Schleppenbach had become involved in the renewal and had invited his cousin from Minnesota to come and visit them for a week to help celebrate his birthday. They hadn't seen Joyce for many years, and they were excited about her coming because she had been deaf and dumb since she was three, and she was now forty-two. They were believing that God would do a miracle for her.

The *Pentecostal Evangel* later reported the miracle that resulted, in their December 14, 1997, issue:

Nothing Is Too Difficult for God
The Deaf Hear

When the Holy Spirit moves, signs and wonders follow. Following is a remarkable story of how God heals those who were deaf today:

Gary Schleppenbach paced anxiously as he awaited his cousin's arrival. Her flight was due any minute. Gary's mind drifted back to the times he and Joyce had played together in Minnesota. Being five years older, he always looked out for her — especially after they discovered, at the age of three, that she was totally deaf in both ears. She was now forty-two, and he wanted to do more for her than "look out for her." He wanted to change her life.

"I'm so excited," Gary said to his wife, Jane. "I just want to lay hands on her right here in the airport and pray for her healing.

Jane smiled. "We will," she said. "The Lord has the perfect time."

After the hugs and greetings, Gary, Jane and Joyce headed for a local discount store to purchase a few necessary items for Joyce's week-long vacation in California. Joyce was disappointed they weren't able to rent a closed-caption television. It was Saturday, and the store's rental department had already closed. Gary told Joyce they'd come back Monday and get one, but inside he was thinking, *I'm glad we couldn't get one because something wonderful is going to happen tomorrow. She won't need a special TV on Monday.*

Gary and Jane had prayed over Joyce's visit for quite some time. He asked his church friends to pray too. For months, Gary faithfully filled out prayer request cards asking that Joyce's ears be opened.

Excitement grew in Gary's heart. "We didn't know if anyone had ever prayed for her healing,"

Gary explains. "And we knew we only had one week and only one Sunday before she went home."

The couple arranged for someone to sign the morning service at Bethel Assembly so Joyce could understand the message. Joyce liked the message so much she stayed for both morning services. She couldn't wait until the evening service.

No one was available to sign that night's message, but Gary wrote key words and special testimonies on paper so Joyce could follow along. Two of the testimonies dealt with healing. They touched her heart.

Gary wasn't sure if Joyce had ever asked Jesus to be her Lord and Savior. He and Jane had wanted to minister to Joyce at home, but the Lord spoke to Gary and said, "No. Wait until the church service, that I might receive the glory."

That Sunday night, at the altar, a woman named Celeste led Joyce to the Lord by way of notebook paper. Then Cal Pierce, an elder of the church, asked if anyone had prayed for Joyce's ears. He hadn't known she was deaf. He was simply being obedient to the Holy Spirit.

Cal and several others gathered around Joyce and prayed for her total healing. Joyce went down under the power of the Holy Spirit and lay on the floor for more than an hour while the Holy Spirit performed surgery.

At 10:10 P.M., Joyce heard hand claps while

still on the floor. The prayer warriors helped her up and further tested her hearing. She began pointing to things around her, sounds she was hearing for the first time in her life.

"She was already responding to hand claps behind her head," Gary says. "I thought, *Let's try finger snaps. They are quieter.* And she heard those too and snapped back at me."

After finding out the details of Joyce's healing, Pastor Bill Johnson made an announcement from the pulpit: "Deaf ears were opened here tonight."

"We didn't get to bed until 1:30 that next morning," Gary says. "She didn't want to go to bed because she had too much to hear — the speaker phone, the refrigerator, her own voice — so many things."

Not only did God open Joyce's ears, He also loosed her tongue. The first word she said plainly was, "Gary." She's learning to speak much like a toddler would," says Gary.

"She sang 'Happy Birthday' to me on May 7," Gary brags. "I've got it all on videotape."

Before Joyce's vacation was over, the family visited Golden Gate Park. Once inside, they ventured into the Academy of Science building which featured videos of sea life. The squawks of seagulls and the sounds of sea life filled the room, and Joyce stood in the middle of it all, pointing and clapping and laughing. Gary proudly stood by, explaining to onlookers that Joyce couldn't hear anything one week ago until Jesus healed her. Strangers rushed to her side to congratulate her.

— *reported by Michelle Adams*

I remember laying hands on Joyce, and her being on the floor, slain in the Spirit.

Gary had come over to where I was in the auditorium and told me that his cousin was there visiting and that she had accepted the Lord, and he asked me if I would pray for her. It took me a while to get to her because she was at the other extreme of the large auditorium, and there were many people lying on the floor that I had to get past. What's more, I wasn't sure exactly who I was looking for. It seems that the Spirit drew me to her.

She went down, and while she was "out" on the floor, I was led to put my fingers in her ears and pray. I bound the spirit of deafness and called forth hearing. Then I went back to the other side of the sanctuary and continued praying for people.

After a while, I heard a shout from that other part of the sanctuary and could see that people were very excited about something that was happening over there. When Joyce got up, she told everyone around her that her ears had been opened and that she was hearing music for the first time in nearly forty years.

What a blessing it was to see that God could use ordinary people like me to do such extraordinary things! What an honor and privilege it was to help bring healing to people like Joyce! I loved the feeling and was sure that I wanted to do that more in the future.

Seven

Good-bye, Retirement!

Michelle had not been touched by the renewal like I was. She didn't oppose what I was doing, but she wasn't totally excited about it either. She went with me to the meetings, but her participation was still rather limited. It was, therefore, with a bit of trepidation that she watched me become such a fanatic about the whole thing.

I could sense her reservations when I announced to her one day that we would have to scrap all of our plans for the future. There would be no early retirement and no "RV'ing." That lifestyle no longer interested me in the least. She resigned herself to my decision.

Because of all this, I didn't really expect Michelle to understand when I told her one day that I felt led to take a trip north. I wasn't sure that I understood myself. I asked her if she minded if I would be gone for a few days, suggesting that I needed a few days alone to pray.

"Well, where are you going?" she asked. And I wasn't sure what to respond. My parents had been to Spokane some years before, and at one time we had some relatives there. But that was the only connection I could think of in the area. "I'll probably go up to Spokane for a few days," I told her. She said she didn't mind, as long as I would call her once I got wherever it was I was going.

The truth was that my urge was much more serious than I was admitting to Michelle at the moment. We had grown up in Redding, and we had gone to school, married and raised our family there. We had fully expected to live there the rest of our lives. But recently I had been feeling an unmistakable urge to leave the place. This could not be easily explained, because I was absolutely enthralled with the revival we were experiencing in Redding.

Still, I could not deny what I was feeling. God had given me something, and I had to use it. He was giving me more power every day, and I had to put it to work for Him. Some would say that this was my Macedonian call, and others would say it was my personal Great Commission experience. Whatever you want to call it, God was disquieting my spirit for the place we lived and placing within me a love for a place of which I knew absolutely nothing.

I had been teaching a class each Sunday morning, and I announced that I would not be there the following weekend because I was driving north to Spokane to spend some days in prayer. One of the ladies on the front row that day had recently read a book that Ken and Gloria Copeland published about

John G. Lake, and she spoke up. "That's where John G. Lake was from, and he's buried there." I realized then that I had read this myself many months before, but I had forgotten it and hadn't considered the connection until then.

As I drove from Redding to Spokane, a ten- or twelve-hour drive, I kept thinking about what the lady had said. For some reason, I just couldn't get out of my mind the fact that I was going to the city where John G. Lake had been used so mightily by God.

I remembered other things about John G. Lake and Spokane as I drove. I remembered that he had experienced a hundred thousand documented healings in only five years of ministry in that city and that this had resulted in Spokane being officially declared the healthiest city in the world. Wow! I was going to that very city. The thought brought a sense of awe over me.

There were several things, I decided, that I must see in Spokane. I wanted to see the building where all these miracles happened. The original building had burned some years after Lake's death, but it had been replaced with another building of the same name. I felt a burden to go there and pray.

I wanted to see the tabernacle where John G. Lake had ministered, I wanted to see the home where he had lived, and I wanted to see his grave. I decided to try to find the grave first.

Spokane is a city of 190,000, with more than 400,000 in the immediate area, and I had absolutely no idea where to start looking for the grave of John G. Lake. I took the first off-ramp from the interstate and stopped at a convenience store to buy a map of the city. I looked for cemeteries, and found that there were three large ones and many smaller ones. Where to start? I decided to just pick one and try it. Amazingly, I picked the right cemetery on the first try. When I went into the cemetery visitor's center and asked for the grave of John G. Lake, I was directed right to it, and I was told that it was the most visited grave site in the city.

An amazing awe filled me as I stood at the grave of that great man. He had carried a burden, and I was beginning to feel that same burden. He had received a special anointing, and I too felt that God was giving me something special.

As I stood there that day, the biblical story of Elisha came to mind. He had been so powerful in life that, after he had died, when someone threw the body of another dead man into his tomb, the dead man came to life. If the body of Elisha had possessed such a great anointing, I believed that the body of John G. Lake had too.

Desperate men take desperate measures, and that day in the cemetery in Spokane I lay down on that grave site in the spread-eagle position and began to cry out to God. "God, bring up the anointing of this man to me. Let it rise out of his bones. I want to walk in the same power that he walked in. I want to see the miracles he saw."

What I was doing that day had nothing to do with John G. Lake. I was not idolizing him in any way. I simply wanted what he had. I was seeking after the same thing he had sought after. I wanted to bless the sick and hurting of my day as he had blessed the sick and hurting of his.

There were some men mowing in the cemetery, and I was hoping they wouldn't run over me, but otherwise I didn't care. I was desperate.

When I stood up, I asked the Holy Spirit what it was that these men and women saw that allowed them to walk in that measure of power. He told me that they hadn't needed to see anything and that such power came to them by what they heard. The true power of God flows through us by the faith that comes by hearing, and that changes what we see.

I visited the Lake home at 1523 West Indiana Street, I visited the old tabernacle at Sharp and Lincoln on the north side of Spokane where John Lake had preached in the city, and I went to find the old Rookery Building at 14 North Howard Street downtown, where the Healing Rooms had been located.

Many of the occupants of the building had moved to newer facilities, and some rooms were empty. The building had a deserted air to it. I went up to the third floor, where I remembered the Healing Rooms had been, and I spent some time walking up and down the corridors praying.

The enemy was there that day too. He said to me, "What are you doing here? You're no John G. Lake."

I knew that was true, so I went back out to the grave site and prayed some more under the towering pine that graced the grave.

I spent three days in Spokane praying and then drove back home to Redding.

Eight

Good-bye, Redding!

All the way home to Redding, I kept wondering how I would tell Michelle what I was feeling. God wanted us to move to Spokane, Washington. I don't remember exactly what I said. I do remember that it came as somewhat of a shock to Michelle, but not totally so. She had long ago come to realize that God was doing something with me. She still wasn't excited about it, but she was willing to go along.

She had been working for a time at Montgomery Wards in Redding, and when she told her superiors that she was moving, she was told that she could transfer to a store in the Spokane area. I was sure that God would help me to get some work up there until it became clear why we were in Spokane and what we were to do there.

We quickly put our home and business up for sale, and we advertised a garage sale to get what we could out of our equipment and other belongings we didn't want to move. Within a few months' time, we were ready to load up our furniture in a U-Haul truck, attach our car behind it, and pull out of town. Of course, it wasn't as easy as all that.

Both of our living children were already grown.

Carl was married to Dory, and they lived in the San Francisco area with our two grandchildren, and Jaime Michelle was in college in Sacramento. Both Michelle's parents and mine lived in Redding, and we were saying good-bye to them. We were also saying goodbye to all of our wonderful friends at Bethel Church, and that was a tough one. We were both in tears as we pulled out of town, wondering how we would replace all that we were giving up.

Actually, I made several trips to Spokane before we actually moved there. I needed to find some work to help support us until we found our footing (and I did find such a job — working three days a week supervising the maintenance of state facilities for the State of Idaho). It would require me to drive thirty miles back and forth to Coeur d'Alene, Idaho, but I didn't mind that. I needed to find a suitable place for us to stay, and I also wanted to pray more about God's plan for us in the city.

Since our future was so uncertain, we decided not to try to buy a home at first, but to rent, perhaps a duplex, until we got more settled. I took a newspaper and traveled around the city looking at suitable places, but by late in the day I hadn't found anything I liked. It was getting dark when I came to the last place. It was a duplex in a residential area. I met the owner, and he showed me around.

He was remodeling the side of the duplex he showed me so that his mother could live there. There were still people living in the side he wanted to rent to us, he said, but they would be moving within days into a home they had recently purchased. I liked the house and told him we would take it. When I called Michelle and described it to her, she agreed. It seemed to suit our needs.

Now we were on our way. We said our good-byes to our families, the church had a wonderful send-off for us, and we had the truck loaded and ready to leave town when we received a phone call. It was the owner of the duplex. "Mr. Pierce," he said, "I am very sorry to tell you that the family occupying your side of the duplex did not get out in time. Their financing on the house they bought fell through, and they're not at all sure when they might be able to get a new loan commitment."

As I was relaying to Michelle what the man was saying, I could imagine what was going through her mind. We were ready to move to a strange city, and now we had no place to live. After I hung up, I assured her, "If God is sending us to Spokane, He will give us a place to live. Let's just pray about it and see what happens."

Two hours later, I received another phone call. Someone had given me the name of a Christian businessman in Spokane about a month earlier, and I had called him in regards to some work (before I had taken the job with the State of Idaho). This man had told me that when I got to Spokane, he wanted me to give him a call and we would get together for coffee so we could get to know each other. Now he was on the phone.

"Cal," he said, "I understand that you're getting ready to move to Spokane. The pastor of our church has moved on, and we have our parsonage open. We've been praying that God would send someone who was interested in occupying it. Would you and your wife be interested?"

I said, "Hallelujah, we would."

The day we moved into that parsonage, the local people came out to help us unload and take everything into the house. It was a wonderful start to what may have seemed to some to be an uncertain future. I was sure that God knew just what He was doing.

— Nine —

Gaining Our Footing

We still were not sure exactly why God had sent us to Spokane, but we were determined to find out. When we weren't working our jobs to keep ourselves afloat, we were trying to find our spiritual footing in the area.

One thing I did was to continue to visit the grave of John G. Lake. In fact, I made a point of going there at least once a month for prayer. I didn't always do my praying spread out over the grave, as I had that first time. Sometimes I sat under the large tree near the headstone and prayed, and sometimes I walked up and down the road as I prayed. Most of the time, I was all alone and could be free to seek God for more of His Spirit and for His will for us in that city.

As soon as we arrived in Spokane, we began visiting churches in the area. In fact, sometimes we split up and went separate ways to visit more churches and get to know them. Michelle would go to one, and I would go to another. We were interested in a church home for ourselves, and we were interested in meeting people who knew how to help us pray and find God's will for us in the city.

Finding a church home did not prove to be easy.

We had come out of that wonderful revival in Redding, and it was hard for the churches around Spokane to compete with that experience. We had grown accustomed to services that went on for hours into the night, with wonderful things happening, and that same thing was now hard to find.

In each church we attended, I asked people if they knew about John G. Lake. Most of them did, and they told me that they were praying and believing for that same healing anointing to return to the city. Many of those I met agreed with this sentiment. Each time I had a discussion like this, I would walk away thinking, *My goodness. It's been eighty years now. How much longer do we have to pray?*

In each church we visited, I inquired about prayer meetings. Most of the people told me they had at some former time held prayer meetings, but when the people stopped coming, they stopped having the prayer meetings. I once asked a pastor if I could come and pray all night in his church. He could lock me in at night and come and let me out the next morning. The pastor seemed surprised by this request and said that it was the first time anyone had suggested it. He didn't seem overly enthusiastic about the idea, so I continued my prayerful visits to the cemetery.

I was praying there that fall as the leaves were coming down from the trees. I was praying there that Christmastime in the snow and cold. I was praying there in the spring as the flowers began to push their way up through the soil. And I was praying there in the heat of the next summer.

Time after time I returned home from my solitary vigil and said to my wife, "Honey, I must be the loneliest person in the world. The only place I have to pray is the cemetery." I wasn't sure why my prayers didn't seem to be moving the hand of God. The heavens seemed to be made of brass. But I simply could not give up. I kept pressing and pressing some more.

I knew that God had moved us up to Spokane for a purpose, but I somehow couldn't quite put my finger on what that purpose was. "God," I prayed, "You haven't changed. I know You can do the same things today that You have done in other periods." Even though it wasn't happening at the moment, I went on believing that it would.

After a year and three months of this (I remember that it was February 28), the Holy Spirit prompted me to go on a forty-day fast, from the beginning of Lent to Palm Sunday. I had done some fasting before, but rarely more than two days at a time. Now, I told Michelle that I was going to fast for forty days. "I'm not sure how I will do it," I admitted, "but I must try." And I did.

Michelle and I were both surprised by how well the first week of the fast went, then two, then three and then four, and I was able to finish the forty days. In the final days of the fast, the Holy Spirit began to direct my attention to the book of Genesis and the story of Isaac re-digging the wells that had belonged to his father Abraham. In the intervening years, the Philistines had backfilled the wells, rendering them useless, but now Isaac was restoring them and causing them to again give forth fresh water — for him, his people and his flocks.

I noticed something very important about Isaac's story. He had pitched a tent, built an altar and cried out to God. But then he had taken a second step and gone beyond prayer. Isaac had to act if his vision was to be accomplished. He had to begin to actually re-dig the wells.

When the wells were again dug, Isaac gave them the same names his father had given them. The wells had been restored and were now accomplishing the same service they had in Abraham's day.

The Holy Spirit was telling me that there is a time to pray, and there is a time to act. I couldn't walk on water if I never got out of the boat. If I would begin to walk, the Spirit showed me, God would confirm what I was trying to do for Him. I had to re-dig the wells of healing. I had to begin to put my vision into action.

Also during the final days of the fast, the Lord directed me to go back to the Rookery Building and pray. I still wasn't John G. Lake, but I was getting better acquainted with the God he had served. "If you want to re-dig a well," the Lord said, "you have to go back to the site of that well."

As I climbed the stairs of the Rookery Building and walked up and down the third-floor corridor, I sensed that something had changed. The enemy was now silenced, and the Spirit said to me, "It wasn't John G. Lake who did it. I did it, and I'm still here."

I knew in that moment that I needed to lease some space in that building and call for intercessors who could help me re-dig the wells of healing. It could be done no other way.

We immediately set about to call intercessors from the area to a day of prayer to be held May 29, 1999, a week from that Saturday. We quickly prepared a brochure that described what we would be doing that day, and we got it out to as many people as possible. My purpose in sending such a brochure was not only to find men and women who would have enough of a burden to come and help us pray that one day. Among those who responded, I hoped to find enough anointed people to form our first healing teams to minister to the sick of the area.

— Ten —

The First Healing in Spokane

From the first day we arrived in Spokane, we were believing for miracles of healing upon the sick. How it would happen was not yet clear, but we were sure that God would make a way.

One of the first believers we met in the city was a military man, Pat Deaton. Pat told us that he had hepatitis C. I wanted to pray for him right then, but his church had a policy that only those who had been in the church for at least six months could minister to others. They apparently had some problems with people passing through, and because of it had established this rule. I could respect that.

Five years before we met Pat, a man with an assault rifle had come onto the military base where he worked and started firing. Pat just happened to be in the wrong place at the wrong time, and he was shot in the shoulder. During surgery to remove the bullet and repair the wound, someone had inadvertently given him tainted blood, and he contracted the hepatitis. It was now so advanced that he could barely get up in the morning, and then only with the help of his wife. At thirty-nine, he was facing an almost-certain medical discharge.

I began to share with Pat the promises of healing from God's Word, His divine provision for His children. I assured him that not only was God able to heal him, but that He wanted to do it.

Pat said, "No one has ever said these things to me," and I could see his faith beginning to rise.

Because I was determined to honor the limitations placed on me by the policy of that particular church, I wondered what I should do. "Let me seek God this week about what I should do," I told him. "I know that God wants to heal you. Maybe we can find a way."

The following Sunday, I saw Pat again at church. He came over and asked me, "What did the Holy Spirit say to you?"

I answered, "The Lord said to tell you that within two weeks you will be healed." Although I told him this, and it may have sounded easy to him, it had been a struggle for me to obey. Pat was a member of the board of elders of that church and had been in the church for more than ten years. He was well known in the Christian community. But more than that, everyone in Spokane had read or heard about the shooting at Fairchild Military Base, and I didn't want to get started on a wrong foot by looking like a fool before the whole city.

I said to the Lord, "You tell him," but He insisted that I do it.

Throughout the week, I kept praying to see if there

might be something else I could tell Pat. Finally, when nothing else became apparent, I complained to the Lord, "But what about my reputation?"

The Spirit said to me, "Son, you don't have a reputation here."

"Well, okay then, Lord, I'll tell him," I finally conceded, "but You have to do the healing."

The Lord answered me, "You finally got it right."

No sooner had I told Pat what the Lord had said than he began telling his family and friends. I would have felt better if he had kept this news quiet, and I told him so, but he just couldn't keep it to himself. It wasn't in his nature.

When this story began to spread like wildfire, I felt very pressured and began desperately calling on God. I'm not sure if I was praying more for Pat's healing or for my own future in ministry in the city.

Pat was suddenly very confident and began talking about his healing as a sure thing. "In just one more week," he was saying, "I'm going to be healed." It was apparent that he really believed it, and that made me all the more nervous.

That Thursday, I attended a prayer and praise time at the church. Pat came over to me excitedly and said, "My children are asking me, 'Dad, what day is it you're going to be healed?' " *Oh my*, I thought. *Now his whole family is expecting him to be healed, and any day now.*

I rather dreaded Sunday, but when it came, I saw

and talked with Pat, and nothing was said of his healing. He looked about the same to me. I didn't see any change. I wondered if he had forgotten all about the Lord's deadline of two weeks for his healing.

By Thursday, I still hadn't heard anything from Pat. I went to the service, but I sat as far back in the corner as I could, hoping that no one would see me. Then, toward the close of the service, I saw Pat. He was coming my way, and he had another of the church elders with him.

The suspense was killing me. Was he going to tell me some good news? Or were they coming to re-prove me for my false prophecy? And would I now become the laughingstock of the whole town?

I greeted the two men, and Pat sat down beside me. In the tenseness of the moment, he began, "Cal, I want to tell you what happened. When I got up on Monday, I was feeling really good. I went to the base infirmary and asked them to draw some blood from me and test it. They called me later to say that they wanted to do some further tests. They asked me to come in for a larger blood sample that they could send to an outside lab.

"When those tests came back, I was called into the office of the chief surgeon. He sat me down and began to tell me the results. 'Pat,' he said, 'we've been treating you here now for the past several years, and we have a file on you that is a couple of inches thick. As we told you some time ago, hepatitis C is incurable. If we could stop it, there would always be a residual effect, and a person could never hide the fact that he had it.

" 'I'm telling you all that to say that something very unusual has happened in your case. We can't understand your lab results. We know you had hepatitis C, but the reports came back, in both instances, indicating that you are completely free of the disease.' "

We were all overjoyed with that good news, and no one was more overjoyed than I was. I encouraged Pat to give the Lord the glory by telling everyone what He had done. That Sunday, he did just that in the church, and the place exploded with praise.

A few days later, Pat was at the military base, talking to the commanding general's secretary, and the general happened by. Pat shared with him his testimony of how God had healed him. As the opportunity arose, he shared the story with other officers, and in this way, Jesus was glorified.

God also used Pat and his testimony to spread the news of His goodness to others throughout the community. God was at work in Spokane. Of that, we had no doubt.

— ELEVEN —

OTHERS ALSO PREPARE THE WAY

When I got home late on Tuesday of that next week, Michelle told me that a man from Vancouver, Washington, had been trying to reach me and had called several times. His name, she said, was Timothy Johnson.

I didn't think I knew anyone by that name, but the man had left his phone number and asked that I call him back no matter how late I got in, so I did. The result was an amazing conversation that lasted for the next two hours.

"I recently heard about what you are doing there in Spokane," Tim Johnson told me. "The amazing thing is that God sent me and a friend of mine to that city several times over a period of eighteen months to prepare the way for this ministry." He was right; this was amazing! And I wanted to hear more.

"Tom Benson and I just got back from a healing conference in Canada," he told me. "While we were waiting for the meeting to begin, a man came in and sat down next to me. I introduced myself, and he said he was from Spokane. When I told him that Tom and I had just finished a work in Spokane, he asked what it was. I told him that we had made a series of trips there to prepare for what the Spirit is saying will be a new outpouring of healing upon the city, and he pulled out your brochure and handed it to me. I was amazed."

In August of 1996, Tim and Tom had attended a meeting in Spokane conducted by a well-known prophet named Bob Jones. Bob had prophesied that a new healing anointing would begin outside the city of Spokane, would then be brought into the city, and would eventually go out from here to all the world. Tim and Tom believed the prophecy and were willing to do anything necessary to bring it about.

About the same time God was bringing Michelle and me into the city of Spokane, He also brought Timothy Johnson and Tom Benson. They came here from Vancouver, Washington, to prepare for the healing anointing that would be poured out in the city and then taken to the world.

Of course, there was much more to it than that. These men made some great sacrifices to obey the Lord so that His blessing could come upon Spokane. Each of the trips Tim and Tom made into Spokane had taken them at least seven and a half hours each way, and they also had gone on several lengthy fasts, believing for the city. They too had been led to go to the grave of John G. Lake to pray, and they too had prayed at the Rookery Building. The Spirit had said to them, "I am sending you to prepare the way for healing." Every six months or so from the time of that first burden, they had done another forty-day fast and gone into Spokane for several days of prayer.

This was amazing. These men didn't know us, and we didn't know them, yet God had dealt with each of us separately concerning the exact same burden. How wonderful!

Timothy began to share with me in rapid-fire order many of the other things that had happened to the two of them on these trips.

"The first thing Bob Jones told us about during that conference was what he saw in the spirit realm as he prepared for the meetings in Spokane. He saw a huge python over the city. He was given the authority to strike the python behind its head with a sword, but he couldn't kill it. The Lord told him that the local church would have to do that. He then struck it in the reproductive organs so that it could not reproduce before the church got united enough to kill it.

"He also saw the angel God had set over the area, and that angel was tattered because he had been in intense battles with demonic forces, with very little assistance. God's people needed to unite in intercession, he declared, so that more angelic forces would be sent to the area.

"In the months before we first went to Spokane to hear Bob Jones, we began hearing reports of the ministry of John G. Lake. Until then, we had never heard of the man. Now everywhere we went people were stirred by several new books about Lake's life and ministry, and many were believing for the anointing that gave him such success in Spokane to return to the city.

"I bought one of those books and read it, and my heart was also challenged. Before we left home for the conference in Spokane, the Lord told us to go visit John Lake's grave while we were in the city. There the Lord spoke to me and said, 'I will restore the healing anointing that was on John G. Lake. It will start in Spokane and spread like wildfire across America from here. Revival in the Northwest will also begin in Spokane.' I sensed that the roots of the huge pine tree over the grave were flowing down into the bones of the man of God and bringing up strength for a new generation of healing ministers.

"That evening we were totally 'blown away' when Bob Jones told us that when he got off of the plane in Spokane, the Lord had spoken to him to go to the John G. Lake grave and pray. He said the Lord had revealed to him that the tree growing down into the grave was a prophetic sign from God that He would revive the anointing that had been over this servant. He saw the cones from the pine tree as a symbol of the seed that would now multiply. This new anointing, Bob Jones declared, would be tenfold greater than anything previously experienced.

"Once," Tim told me, "when we had finished our fast, I asked God if it was time for us to go to the city, and He said it was. I called Tom and asked him if he could go with me. He said it was a very busy time for him, and he wasn't sure he could go. I suggested that he pray about it during the week and ask God what he should do. If the Lord confirmed it to him, we would go on Saturday."

Tom began to pray, and the Holy Spirit said to him, "Go into the garage and get the staff you cut in the redwood forest in the Valley of the Giants a few months ago. Bring it into the house and write on it My name, Elohim." Tom thought that was a very strange thing to do, but he obeyed.

"Now," the Spirit urged when he had finished doing that, "call Tim and tell him you will go with him." When Tom related to Tim what God had just told him to do, he was amazed to find that Tim was sitting at his own kitchen table with a staff that he had just finished writing the names of God on. It seemed that God was trying to tell them both something. The men took their staffs with them when they went to Spokane that weekend and used them as they marched around the areas God showed them to intercede for.

When the Lord sent them to the Rookery Building the very first time, they walked around the area praying. As they passed through a food court on the opposite side of the street from the building, they encountered a demonic force that nearly knocked them off their feet. Tim told me, "I seemed to be suddenly overtaken by a magnetic field, and I had the feeling of static electricity around my body. Something felt very cold and grossly evil. I cannot describe how hideous and demonic this presence felt to me. Thomas felt it too, and asked me, 'What is this?'

"We went on to another part of the downtown, and when we returned and passed by that way again, we felt the same thing as before. Tom felt that we had encountered a prince of demons over the city, and he sensed the arrogance and mockery of the demon, as he seemed to boast, 'This is my city, and I will not be brought down.' " We would see about that.

"On New Year's Eve of 1997, my wife and I invited some prophetically gifted friends to our house for prayer. God revealed many wonderful things to us that night. After our prayer time, Tim slept over at our house, and the next morning we were discussing a dream I had concerning the coming healing revival in Spokane. Over and over I kept hearing a word from the Lord about 'a lake of medicine.' We got out a map of the Spokane area and looked for anything like that, but nothing seemed to pop out at us.

"Then my wife, Betty, found a better map, and we were amazed at what we discovered on it. Just outside of Spokane was a lake clearly marked on the map as Medical Lake. We wondered if this is what Bob Jones' prophecy had meant. The revival of healing would start outside of Spokane. Would it come from Medical Lake?

"We went to the computer and looked on the Internet to see if we could find anything about Medical Lake. We learned that Medical Lake was also the name of a small town, five miles outside of Spokane, on the shores of Medical Lake. The lake was discovered by a French Canadian sheepherder by the name of Lefever. In the early 1800s, he had gone to the lake one day to bathe and was immediately healed of his advanced rheumatoid arthritis. He had named the lake in French, and his name translated to Medical Lake.

"Local Indians had also discovered the medicinal and curative powers of the water of Medical Lake. They had built steam baths around the lake, where they poured the water over hot rocks and breathed in the resulting steam. They also claimed many healings from its use.

"The water of Medical Lake was found to be high in mineral content, so that when it was boiled down, it left a salty residue. The Indians carried these salts to distant tribes who could not reach the lake, and many of them likewise claimed healing from the use of the salts.

"In April of that year, the Lord impressed upon us to again undertake a long fast. He was about to send us back to Spokane. We didn't know what all we would be doing, but one thing the Lord showed us was that we would speak a word of release over the city. We were then to end our fast in Spokane.

"As we drove into the city, we could not help but notice how many hospitals and clinics there were. We looked for a good map and did a better survey of this phenomenon. A city that had once been declared "the healthiest city in America" was now obviously a place of much sickness.

"This time, we were determined to learn more about the demonic force we had both felt near the town center. The first time we approached that particular food court where we had felt it before, sure enough, there it was again. After we had gone back to our hotel room, we began to seek God as to whom we were up against.

"Tom opened his Bible to the story of David and Goliath and read it out loud, and I asked him to read it again, slower this time. As he read it once again, we felt the Lord telling us that it was the spirit of Goliath that had spread intimidation over the city of Spokane and prevented the healing anointing from flowing back into it.

"A few minutes later, we decided to go out again to a mall to buy something. On the way, our eyes were drawn to a billboard. It read: BURGER HUT — HOME OF THE GOLIATH BURGER. God was confirming to us what He had spoken only moments before.

"That night, the Lord spoke to us to go out to

Medical Lake the next morning for the first time. We prayed around the lake and were led to thrust our staffs into it to 'trouble' the water. We felt sure that the moment we put our staffs in, there was a 'stirring of the waters.' Tom was weeping, as the Lord showed him that the healing water of the lake would not be just for Spokane, but for the healing of the nations.

"As a prophetic act, we took five gallons of water from the lake and carried it to a spot where we could pour it into the Spokane River. The river then carried it into the city. As we poured the water into the river, Tom was overcome with emotion and declared, 'This healing will flow to all the nations of the earth.'

"While we were eating in a local restaurant that night, we sensed that we had one more thing to do. We must prophesy to the giant spirit over the city of Spokane the next day, and then we would be free to go home.

"We overheard some ladies in an adjoining booth speaking about a meeting being conducted locally. It was obvious that they were Spirit-filled, so we spoke to them. We were very pleased and surprised to find that they were Spirit-filled Catholics. We had heard about what God was doing among the Catholics, but we had never actually met any Spirit-filled Catholics.

"These ladies were from Montana and had come to Spokane to attend a healing conference at

Gonzaga University. This would be the final night of the conference, and there would be special prayer for anointing and healing. They invited us to attend.

"Well, this sounded like a wonderful opportunity to us. We could share our anointing with the Catholics. After all, they really needed it, didn't they? We decided to go.

"We arrived at the meeting that night with many ideas about how we could be of service to our brethren. What happened next amazed us. The worship portion of the service was awesome, and the longer it went on, the more conviction we felt for having judged our Catholic brothers so wrongly. The anointing in that room was powerful, and they hardly needed any help from us.

"The Lord spoke to us that night: 'What I am about to do here is bigger than just the Protestants or just the Catholics. It will encompass the entire Body of Christ.' It would be this renewed spirit of unity that would topple Goliath.

"At the end of the evening, we were among those lined up waiting to be anointed by the priests. As they laid hands on all of us, people went down under the power of God in every direction. There were bodies covering the entire floor of that auditorium. Tom and I were drunk in the Spirit and felt ready for our most important work the following morning.

"The next morning, we parked in front of the

Rookery Building. We intended to take care of our business with Goliath and then take each other's picture in front of the famous building before leaving town. We stood facing the building as we raised our staffs and spoke forth the word of the Lord against the enemy that bound the city. We declared liberty for the city and that it would once again become a city of healing, a city of refuge and a city of deliverance for all who were oppressed. Then we struck our staffs seven times against the pavement.

"Was it done? Well, all we knew was that we had done our part, and the rest was up to God. As we were leaving, Tom saw a sign two blocks down. It read: DAVID'S PIZZA, and on it was a rendering of Michelangelo's "David." Within twenty minutes of our receiving the revelation of Goliath, the Lord had given us a confirmation, and now, within such a short time after speaking to the giant, God had again confirmed to us that the giant would fall. We left Spokane rejoicing.

"Six months later, the Lord spoke to Tom about a small Catholic church in Medical Lake. We couldn't be sure if there was one there or not, but something was troubling his spirit. We began another forty-day fast, and during that time Tom asked a friend of his if she knew anything about a Catholic church in Medical Lake. She learned that there not only was a very old Catholic church in Medical Lake, but that it conducted two healing services each month. She felt that this was very unusual.

"When I heard this, I called Information for the church in Medical Lake and called to ask when the next healing service would be conducted. I was surprised to learn that it would be on the evening of the fortieth day of my fast. God's timing could not be better!

"A few days before we left for Medical Lake, the Lord gave me a special verse and told me it was for the Catholic priest at Medical Lake. We had planned to go into Spokane and find a room as before, then return to Medical Lake for the Saturday night service. But on the way the Lord told me we should go into Medical Lake that same night — even though it would be quite late when we arrived there. I didn't say anything at the time to Tom. About twenty minutes later, he said to me, 'I think the Lord is speaking to me about going into Medical Lake tonight.'

"When we arrived in Medical Lake about 9:30 that night, we found the Catholic church (on Lake Street). Everything seemed to be dark as we walked around it, but there was a light in an adjoining apartment building, and we went to the door and knocked.

"A middle-aged man answered and introduced himself as Father Tom Mele. We sat down with him and began to tell him how the Lord had led us to his front door. We were not sure how he would receive the stories of our revelations and prophecies, but we held nothing back.

"When we had covered most of the story, I told him that God had given me a message for him. 'This is it,' I said: 'Eye hath not seen, nor ear heard, neither has it entered into your heart, Father Tom, the things He has prepared for you because you love Him.' In that moment, a most amazed expression came over his face, and he excused himself for a moment.

"We could hear him riffling through some papers in the other room, and when he came back, he had a card in his hand. 'Let me explain,' he said. 'Today is the twentieth anniversary of my ordination as a priest. I had entered the ministry because of a promise God gave me, and the day I was ordained I handed out to my friends a card with that promise printed on it. Here, this is one of the original postcards printed twenty years ago. To our amazement, printed on that card were the exact words I had just quoted to the priest (although I had personalized them).

"Father Tom was so deeply touched by our visit that we all got on our knees and prayed together. We were pleased to hear him praying in the Spirit, in other tongues.

"We stayed in a motel closer to Medical Lake that night, and the next day we went into town. It was the last day of our fast, and I was hungry for a hamburger. 'Let's go get one of those Goliath hamburg-ers,' I said to Tim, and we headed in that direction.

" 'I wouldn't be surprised if "Goliath Burger" is shut down,' Tim said as we were nearing the place. Less than a minute later, we could not believe what we were seeing. The concrete structure had been de-molished, and all that was left was a pile of rubble. The Lord said to us, "What you see here in the natu-ral is what took place in the Spirit." We went back to the area around the Rookery Building to see if we could feel a difference, and that horrible power we had felt on our previous visits was now gone. Be-cause we couldn't eat Goliath burgers to break our fast, we settled for David's pizza instead. It was de-licious.

"The meeting at the Catholic church in Medical Lake was great, and the church secretary gave us a copy of an old book on the one-hundred-and-fifty-year history of the church. The book contained a quote from a minister saying, 'Medical Lake in the state of Washington is a modern-day Pool of Bethesda.'

"After we got back home, we looked up the mean-ing of the word *Bethesda*. It means 'house of mercy.' The original Pool of Bethesda is located beside Saint Anne's church in Jerusalem. Now God had opened an American version, not far from that little Catho-lic church in Medical Lake, Washington. The name of that church is also Saint Anne's. Wow!"

After one more fast and one more trip to Spokane, the Lord told Tim and Tom that their part in the work to establish the healing flow once again in the city was finished. As Timothy was telling me these stories, I felt like my hand had accidentally been stuck into a light socket. God was doing something powerful!

That Saturday night, after we had finished our day of re-digging the wells of healing, Tim called me at home. "What did you do?" he asked. I thought he was asking about our day of prayer, and I began to tell him about it, but he said, "No, no! I mean what did you do after I told you about Medical Lake?"

He was right. I had done something. I had driven out to the lake at the earliest possible moment. I had to go. I couldn't stand not to see the place and investigate this mystery. And I took some water from the lake home with me.

"That's what I needed to hear," he said. "The Holy Spirit said through the prophecy given by Bob Jones that the anointing for healing would start outside the city, come into the city and then go around the world. You had to go out there and get that water and bring it back into the city so that the healing anointing could begin. And just as you have started well, I am sure that this anointing will eventually go out around the world."

In our Healing Rooms we keep a vase containing water from Medical Lake. We have come to call it fire water, because when we touch people with it, they say it feels hot to them. It isn't hot in the natural, but it apparently is in the Spirit. We anoint those who come to our Healing Rooms with oil, as the Bible teaches, but when we do conferences, we impart with Medical Lake water.

It was only three weeks after the Lord had told Tim and Tom that their part in the work of preparing the way was completed that someone placed in their hands our brochure about re-digging the wells of healing. They, and some others like them, had sown some powerful seeds of faith in the city, and we were believing for them to bring forth a great harvest.

Twelve

Re-digging the Wells

After we had prepared and sent out the brochure to as many contacts as we could in the area, inviting everyone to come for a day of intercession and re-digging the wells, that was about all we could do for the moment. We had to trust God to do the rest.

Our plan was to spend the day with those who came together, praying at the grave site of John G. Lake, at his former home, at the old tabernacle where his church had been just before he died and at the Rookery Building where the Healing Rooms had been located. Together, we would toss out all the doubt and unbelief that had clogged the former wells, and we would believe God to again show forth His power as He had eighty years before. We knew that He hadn't changed in those eighty years, and we were sure that He would, once again, help us bring healing to the sick of the area.

We believed the prophecy given by Bob Jones was from God. He had also spoken to Michelle and me and to Tim and Tom. God was not finished with Spokane. The healing anointing poured out there in the early part of the past century would return, and the Lord would be glorified again in that place. Some had not been quick to embrace this prophecy, but it was obvious to us that God had been working through many different people to bring it to pass.

As we thought back on it, the prophecy was given in January of 1996, and that was the same month Bill Johnson had come to Bethel Assembly of God Church in Redding to launch the revival that would so drastically impact our own lives. God had also been preparing Tim and Tom to do their part in preparing the atmosphere over the city for the wells of healing to be restored. How amazing that God had begun to set in place several years before all of the details to make this day successful!

Now, we were approaching the crunch time. I knew that intercessory prayer would be the key of any future success in the healing ministry God had destined for the city, and we were about to begin that on a much larger scale.

The day of prayer started off very well. More than a hundred prayer warriors responded to our invitation. They had come not only from Spokane, but from other parts of Washington State, and also from Oregon, Idaho, Montana, and as far away as Utah. Together we visited the grave site, the Lake home and the old tabernacle, and we finished our day in the Rookery Building.

I had spoken to the owners of the building about the possibility of leasing some space, but we had not yet been able to reach a final agreement and to come up with the needed funds. They were kind enough to give me the keys and let us use some rooms for that special day. I wanted everyone to be able to get inside those rooms, and we did — well, sort of. We joined hands in a human chain of prayer that wound in and out of four rooms and in and out of the corridor. At one point, I went down the line, anointing each person in the chain with water from Medical Lake. Many of them were slain in the Spirit.

Three of the rooms were carpeted in a brown tone, but the last room down the hall had a silver carpet. When I got into what came to be called the Silver Room, I found that everyone was on the floor already, and I anointed them right where they were.

Two days later, I received a letter from a woman who had been there that day. "I want to share with you what happened," she began. "I was the first one into that room with the silver carpet. When I entered the room, I simply couldn't stand up, and I fell onto the floor. Then, everyone who came in after me fell too — because the anointing was so powerful.

"At one point, a young lady came through the door. I could literally see the infirmity in her body, and I called it out and told her she was healed in the name of Jesus. She fell down weeping onto the floor, delivered."

I thought about that letter for a long time, and I had it in my pocket several days later when we started to move things into the building. Michelle and I had held a yard sale and sold off whatever we could of our own things to make the first lease payment. Among the things that were sold in those days was all my sporting equipment. I was soon to be very busy for the Lord, and would no longer need it or have time for it.

After I had set down some boxes I had carried in, I thought to myself, *I must go into that Silver Room to see what this lady is talking about.* I went down the hallway and into the room with the silver carpet. When I walked through the door, it was like going through a curtain of anointing. I could feel the presence of God like I had never felt it before. Was I imagining this? I didn't think so.

I went back out to the reception area and then turned and went back to that room again. Actually, I did this several times, and each time I walked through that doorway, it was like going through a curtain. I did this over and over for fifteen or twenty minutes.

The following day, I was again moving some boxes into the room, and I asked the Lord, "What is it that makes the anointing so powerful in that room?"

The Lord answered, "I left an angel in that room, and he has been waiting now for eighty years for the rooms to be reopened for prayer. As long as My angel is there, this healing anointing will be poured out from this place and will go around the world. "

After the Healing Rooms were reopened, more than six hundred pastors would make their way into that room, and each time we would ask them what they felt. Invariably, they answered, "The presence of angels."

I shared this story some time later in a conference I was conducting near Seattle, and a lady stood up and said, "That 'young lady' they spoke of was my daughter, Heather. She was only nine at the time. God healed her that day of a bronchial disorder, and she has been well ever since."

Just as He had promised, God was helping us to restore the wells of healing in the city of Spokane. It was with much rejoicing that we made our way home that night. Wells had been opened, and it was now time for their water to be poured forth.

THIRTEEN

THE REOPENING OF THE ROOMS

After that special day of prayer, we had felt the release to go into action to begin bringing the vision of the reopened Healing Rooms to reality. We had signed the lease on the first three rooms on the third floor of the Rookery Building, and we began to furnish them. We also spent more time in those rooms in prayer.

At the same time, I began to recruit and train a team of men and women who could serve in the daily ministry of the Healing Rooms. This, we knew, was very important.

There were several requirements for those who would serve. The most important of these requirements was that the person have a burden for healing. We needed men and women who were willing to pay any price to see the sick healed, who would be willing, if necessary, even to lay down their own lives for others.

In many ways, those we chose were very ordinary people — housewives, plumbers, mechanics, secretaries and business owners — but in other ways they were extraordinary. They were all hungry for more of God and desirous of seeing His power manifested.

I did five classes in preparation for the Healing Rooms ministry. We studied the provision of divine healing as part of our salvation. We studied God's many promises concerning healing for His people. We studied the special anointing that empowers us to minister healing. We studied roadblocks to healing, things that often get in the way of a person's receiving God's promises.

We studied the spiritual authority we have as Spirit-filled believers and the baptism of the Holy Spirit that seals us and enables us to flow in God's power. We would be dealing with people who were tormented by demon spirits, and we needed to have the authority to put those demons in their place.

Finally, we studied the process we had felt led to establish for the Healing Rooms. Many came to these classes, and from these hungry people we were able to form a small team of anointed prayer warriors. On July 22, 1999, not sixty days after we had met to re-dig the wells of healing, we officially opened the Healing Rooms and began to pray for the sick who came.

Those three rooms we began with gave us only about eight hundred square feet, and we had only eight to ten faithful intercessors who showed up daily to minister. These faithful few were from a variety of denominations, and it was wonderful to see them all coming together in humility and working together in unity for a common purpose.

Because we were all just ordinary men and women, we had to recognize that it was the presence of the Lord Jesus that would do the healing work, and that we could do the extraordinary things He had called us to do only if He was there with us. Therefore, we developed the habit of praying together each morning before the Healing Rooms opened. We conducted these unified prayer times in the Silver Room. Then, after prayer, we got ready to receive sick people and minister healing to them.

One of the first people we prayed for was twenty-year-old Korey Mosher. I had received an e-mail from Korey's mother describing her condition. Korey had osteosarcoma, bone cancer. Eight inches of her femur had been removed and replaced with a piece of bone from a cadaver. That first cadaver bone broke, and doctors had replaced it with another. Now, that bone was also deteriorating, and doctors wanted to remove Korey's leg. Her father, a pastor, would be bringing her to us on Thursday. The team got ready for her in prayer.

We found Korey to be a delightful young lady, and our team prayed over her Thursday morning, Thursday afternoon, Friday morning and Friday afternoon. This was not one continuous prayer. She was prayed for in various rooms and by various team members. On Saturday morning and again on

Saturday afternoon, we prayed for Korey, laying hands on her again. Then we all hugged her and sent her home.

Korey didn't actually look any different when she left us than she had when she came, but a week later I received a phone call informing me that something had, indeed, happened. Korey told me, "After we were home for a few days, I went back to my doctor and asked if he would authorize a new bone scan. He agreed. After he had read the bone scan, he called me into his office and sat me down. He said, 'Korey, you're going to make a believer out of me yet. That dead bone has somehow come to life.' "

How happy we were to hear this wonderful news! That one miracle was worth it all. Korey having back her life was worth any commitment we could possibly make. This was what we were giving our lives for.

In the first weeks the Healing Rooms were open, as word got out about what God was doing in downtown Spokane, we were all there praying only two days a week — Thursdays and Fridays. Even then, we were not terribly busy. It didn't take long, however, before people were arriving unannounced from all over the city and the state. Then people began walking in the door and saying they were from Virginia, Texas, Colorado or some other part of the country. We would ask if they were in Spokane for some other reason. "No," they said. Someone had told them about what we were doing or they had stumbled across our website, and they had been led to come for prayer.

Many of the people who came to us for prayer were in a desperate physical condition. So many desperate ones came in so quickly, in fact, that it drove us to our knees in prayer. These people were dying, and they were depending on our prayers to help them. Our morning prayer times became moments of absolute desperation and deep crying out to God. Without Him, we could do nothing.

I can never forget what I saw in the Silver Room on those mornings. Men and women were on their faces before God, weeping and saying, "Oh, God, You must come. You must do the work." We had no choice but to cry out. We needed miracles from Heaven. Men and women were coming because we had invited them and had told them that God was still God and He had not changed. Now, in one sense of the word, we were responsible for the healing of these critically ill patients.

Our desperation increased as people from other countries heard about the Healing Rooms and got on a plane and came for prayer. We had people from Singapore, Great Britain, Australia and South Africa, as well as from many parts of Canada and from all over the United States.

We were in awe of what God was doing. That He would pour out His Spirit so powerfully through ordinary people like us revealed His greatness even more.

The process we established for the Healing Rooms worked well. We would have a small team, usually with three members, to pray in each of the Healing Rooms. One of the team members would act as the leader, and the others would follow his or her lead, agreeing in prayer and cooperating with the ministry that was indicated by the Spirit.

When the sick people arrived, they would be received at the reception area, and there they would fill out forms very similar to those used in doctors' offices. Each person would give his or her name, address, phone number and church affiliation. There were boxes to check for the questions "Are you born again?" and "Are you filled with the Holy Spirit?" Then there was space to describe their physical problem.

This information sheet was then passed to one of the available prayer teams. The members of the team took it into the particular room where they were assigned to minister, laid their hands on it and agreed together that the work would be done.

We have always believed very strongly in the biblical promise:

> *If two of you agree on earth about anything that they may ask, it shall be done for them by My Father who is in heaven.*　　　Matthew 18:19

There is power in unity. The Bible speaks of one chasing *"a thousand"* and two putting *"ten thousand to flight"* (Deuteronomy 32:30). This is the reason we wanted three praying together in each room, and we noticed the difference if there were only two of us at any one time.

As the team members prayed over the information sheet of each new sick person, they were also seeking God for a particular healing strategy. They would soon see the person, but only after the explosion of anointing that came through their prayer time together and only after they had some confirmation about how to proceed with the ministry to that person. In this way, the ministry would never become just another routine. Each sick person was a new challenge, and we were determined to find God's unique answer for each one.

The prayer teams quickly became very gifted in this regard. As we all prayed six to eight hours a day in the Healing Rooms and walked in obedience to the Holy Spirit, we began to experience a flow of all nine of the gifts of the Spirit in our midst. Even though our particular calling was with the gifts of healing, all of the gifts were there, available to minister to the sick. Many of the team members began to speak out words of knowledge, as the Spirit revealed to them something about the sick person or the sickness involved and what was necessary to overcome it. This proved to be a powerful ministry tool.

From the beginning, we were not very much interested in counseling those who came for our prayers. Instead, we wanted to see God deliver them and make them whole again. We also did not spend much time with "deliverance" (as we had known it in the past). Our emphasis was not on demons, but on the presence of the Holy Spirit. If His anointing did not come to break the yokes of sickness and oppression and set the people free, we could pray all day and nothing would happen. If His presence was in the Healing Rooms, sickness would have to flee. This became the great secret of our success.

Far too often, people have sought healing without seeking God. We have sought His hand and not His face. If we go after the Healer and not the healing, then we have Him with us always. Just as those who come face-to-face with the Savior get saved, those who come face-to-face with the Healer are healed.

We did see the manifestation of evil spirits. One Saturday morning, for instance, during the morning prayer time with our team, I was led to tell them to get ready because we were going to see someone actually be lifted off the floor that day by evil spirits. Later that day, one team was praying with a man who had come. They had him sitting in the middle of the room, and suddenly a demon spirit began to manifest itself.

A lady in the team pointed at the sick man and

said, "You spirit of deception, you come out in Jesus' name!" As she did this, she shook her finger at him and then she used that finger to fling the spirit out of him toward the wall.

The spirit in that man was not happy about coming out of his "house," and he pulled the man up out of his chair, flung him across the room and landed him spread-eagle against the wall. In all of that, the man never touched the floor. When he did fall to the floor, he was totally delivered. We have seen many other unusual demon manifestations. The enemies of Christ get desperate when they know they have to come out.

The miracles that began to take place daily in the Healing Rooms are best understood by personalizing them, putting a name with the glorious details. These miracles were happening because God loved people and wanted to demonstrate His power on their behalf.

For instance, I will never forget the day Brian Wilkes came for prayer. Only in his mid-thirties, Brian had already undergone two brain surgeries to remove cancerous tumors and had received the required follow-up chemotherapy. But the cancer had returned, and doctors had now given up on him, saying that he had only six months to live. Brian was touched the day he came for prayer, and he came back for additional prayer on other days. Within weeks, a brain scan showed that Brian's tumor had shrunk to the size of a pea, and it was no longer cancerous.

Another wonderful testimony, and one that was widely circulated, came from Kim Eldridge of West Chester, Ohio:

"On May 16, 1998, I awakened, unable to move the right side of my body. Very healthy at twenty-four, I had no idea what was happening. After three days of tests, the doctors said I had had a stroke caused by a blood clot released from my heart. Over the next several months, I worked hard to regain control of my right arm and leg, relearning everything — how to walk, eat, write and drive.

"Six months to the day after the stroke, I was hospitalized again. Pericarditis, an inflammation of the lining surrounding the heart, was the initial diagnosis. After several tests, more specialists and two months, the diagnosis was systemic lupus, an autoimmune disease that attacks healthy cells in any part of the body, including the major organs. Other symptoms included extreme fatigue, sun sensitivity and lupus arthritis in all the joints of my body.

"The next two years brought several health challenges. Most importantly, the lupus attacked the lining of my stomach. Eating and drinking were impossible without extreme pain. The doctor prescribed a narcotic pain killer four times a day that made it possible to eat and function normally.

"In June 2000, my parents wanted to take me to the Healing Rooms in Spokane, Washington. They were convinced that I had a healing in my future. The only reason I agreed to go was because it was a free trip and I had never been to the Pacific Northwest. Sure, I had seen many healings, even in my father. However, I did not believe there was a healing for me.

"We arrived at the Healing Rooms early on Tuesday. I could feel the presence of the Holy Spirit as soon as I walked into the waiting area, and I began to suspect that something good was in store for me.

"We had had such a difficult time getting there: two of our flights were delayed, our anticipated travel time tripled, and my luggage was lost for thirty-six hours. The luggage contained my twelve medications. To top it all off, the air conditioning was broken at the first hotel we checked into and we had to move.

"I received prayer the first day in the Silver Room, a small room with silver carpet, where a healing angel had been waiting for the rooms to be reopened since John G. Lake and his healing teams had used the same location eighty years earlier. The presence of the Holy Spirit was awesome. The only thing I could do was lie on the floor. Still, I did not feel like I had been healed.

"The second day I experienced even less. On the third day, the prayer team leader asked my parents and me what we wanted. I told him I wanted two things — no more stomach pain and discernment to hear from the Lord in a way that I had experienced in the past. He said the discernment was easy and that he would pray against confusion.

"He placed his hands on my ears, and I felt great power in my head. Then I heard a loud pop. When he took his hands away, I felt like my ears had been opened. I could now hear sounds from the open window that I had not heard previously. This was strange, because there had not been a physical hearing problem. I believe that my mind and spirit were opened, and this manifested in my hearing more clearly.

"The second request was next. I was still experiencing terrible pain. In fact, the pain had gotten worse since I arrived in Spokane. The prayer team leader told the pain to leave in the name of Jesus Christ. And it left! I was so amazed by this that I was left speechless.

"We finished the prayer time, and I told my parents that I was going down the street to get something to eat. As soon as I ate, the pain returned. I went back to find the man who had

97

prayed for me and told him the pain was back. He prayed again, and it left again! He then explained to me that I needed to take the authority God had given me and tell the pain to go. That evening I stopped taking the narcotic painkillers prescribed for me, and I prayed for strength to fight my sickness.

"Over the next week, a pattern emerged. The pain would come back, and I would pray it away. It would come back, and I would pray it away again. My family joined me as I continued to pray.

"Eventually, I got angry at the pain. How dare it continue to attack me, a child of the King of Kings, Lord of Lords! I said, 'This is it! This is the last time you will afflict me! Get out of here in the name of Jesus and don't come back!'

"The pain came back one more time as if to say, 'Ha! Are you challenging me?' But the Lord got the last laugh. I prayed again, and the pain left me for good. I was healed! My healing first manifested on June 30, 2000, in Spokane, and within two weeks, the battle over the pain continually returning was over. It would have been very easy to give up at the first sign of the pain attempting to return. I have learned that we sometimes have to fight in the Lord to maintain our healing.

"More important than the physical healing, I

received an emotional healing. My first love was back. Before I went to Spokane, anger and depression over my situation had killed any intimacy I had ever experienced with the Lord. I was so lonely and desperate that I didn't know how to reach out to Him. I ran from everyone who loved me.

"Now I know that we can't outrun our Lord. He keeps us in His sights, no matter where we try to hide. I thank Him for my healing every day. Most of all, I thank Him for drawing me back into His presence. He has assured me that He was always there, but now I live in His presence."

Kim, the youngest daughter of Darrel and Marilyn Eldridge, pastors of Father's Heart Christian Fellowship, a Partners In Harvest (PIH) church, in West Chester, Ohio, is a theatre teacher and director for Lakota West High School in West Chester, a north suburb of Cincinnati. You can be sure that her miracle has touched many lives.

Even though healing miracles like these are a demonstration of God's love for the individual who has been sick, they serve a much larger purpose. The whole world needs to see the miracles of God. Everyone needs to hear these kinds of testimonies. Miracles are often God's tools for bringing lost people to Himself, and miracles play a very important role in bringing revival to those who already know God, but may have grown cold.

More than six thousand sick people were ministered to in the Healing Rooms during our first twenty-one months of operation. Within a year and a half, we had ten rooms in operation and a team of seventy-five anointed men and women ministering four days a week in those anointed rooms.

Could a person be healed? Well, we would never know if we didn't lay hands on him or her and believe for healing. God had promised it, and we just needed to do what was necessary to claim it.

Not long ago, I received a letter from Korey Mosher's sister. She said, "At Mom and Dad's twenty-fifth wedding anniversary, Korey (whom the doctors said would never dance again) stood and danced for them." What a blessing it was for us to hear that!

In the Healing Rooms, we now have a "Wall of Healing." It is covered with cards containing the testimonies of those who have been healed. We receive such cards every day. When would we reach a hundred thousand documented healings, as John G. Lake and his fellow believers did? We had made a good start, and the rest was up to the Lord.

— Fourteen —

The Burden for Downtown Spokane

About six months after we opened the Healing Rooms, I heard about a meeting being held each week on the top floor of the Double Tree Hotel in downtown Spokane to pray over the city. The manager's name was Denny Fitzpatrick, and I felt like I needed to meet him. When I was finally able to meet Denny, he shared what God was doing through the prayers of those who were meeting with him.

The Lord had put on his heart a burden to get together a dozen businessmen who would begin to "prayer walk" the downtown area. He and the others who were meeting began praying that they could find these twelve individuals. Once they found the people they wanted, they decided to map out a specific area of the downtown and to systematically claim it for God. They took a map of the downtown area and drew four lines on it, marking off the section the Lord had showed them as their prayer responsibility. They were determined to drive a spiritual stake at each corner of that area and to begin reclaiming it for God.

One of the men suggested that they have a city

engineer who was also a believer calculate for them where the exact center of the marked area was so that they could drive a spiritual stake there as well. After the engineer had studied their map, he told them, "The exact center of the area you marked is right across the street from the Double Tree. It's within the confines of a restaurant called The Mustard Seed." This was the same spot where Tim and Tom had finished their final fast for the city. They were able to get the permission of the owner of The Mustard Seed to actually drive a stake to mark the center of the downtown area.

God answers prayer, and He is now pouring out His Spirit all over the city of Spokane. A city that was once considered by many pastors to be too difficult to evangelize is now experiencing a mighty move of God.

Spokane has not yet been officially proclaimed the healthiest city in this century, but God is working. As Tim and Tom had noticed, nowadays there are many hospitals and clinics in Spokane, and the city has been known for its medical centers, not its place for divine healing. But that is quickly changing. In a recent newsletter, George Otis, Jr., listed some cities God has been saying He will use mightily, and Spokane was at the top of the list.

The atmosphere over the city has already changed. God has spoken about what He intends to do in this city, and now the church is responding in the realization that we can indeed take our city for Him. God's desire is that every city of America be taken by His power of the Holy Spirit through the work of His warriors.

One of our local newspapers, *The Spokesman's Review*, sent a writer and a photographer to spend three weeks monitoring what was happening here in the Healing Rooms and to issue reports on it. *The Spokesman's Review* is the largest newspaper in the inland Northwest, and it reaches half a million readers.

The first feature article appeared at the end of November 2000, on the front page of the paper, with several photos inside. It was a very favorable article, and thus the news is getting out. This was a great blessing, because John G. Lake had his problems with *The Spokesman's Review*. God had given us favor.

Because of that first article, we received a phone call from an administrator at Sacred Heart Hospital here in Spokane. The hospital has what they call a faith healing center. The administrator came to the Healing Rooms to meet us and to observe our operation. Later, he asked me, "Would you permit us to send people here for prayer?" We were more than happy for him to do that and happy that we were making an impact on downtown Spokane.

Fifteen

The Expansion of the Vision to Other Cities and Nations

When it became apparent just how successful the reopened Healing Rooms were becoming, I began to receive invitations from around the country to teach conferences on healing. Before long, we were doing two such conferences each month, and I was booked a year in advance.

When I go out to these conferences, I do so with the assurance that we have a wonderful team that continues the ministry of the Healing Rooms while Michelle and I are away. That not only frees me to go; it gives me great consolation that the system we have put in place in Spokane is working. Usually, six or eight of our team members from the Spokane Healing Rooms also accompany us to the conferences to help minister to the people who attend.

To each of these conferences, we take with us some water from Medical Lake and use it to impart the healing anointing to the Body of Christ in each place. Our hearts' desire is to see the healing power of God become the "norm" for all of our churches and no longer the exception. We rejoice in imparting this anointing to other people just like ourselves, so that they can begin to do the extraordinary things the Lord has promised.

Another thing that quickly began to happen was that men and women were challenged to open Healing Rooms in their own cities. At the time of this writing, there are some fifty other Healing Rooms either established or in the process of being established around the country. Healing Rooms are also being opened in Canada, Australia, New Zealand, England, South Africa, Korea and other parts of the world. All of these Healing Rooms are independently operated. We provide the local believers the tools to work with and help them with training to continue the work. Just as God has worked here in Spokane, He is on the move in other cities around the country and around the world, and testimonies are coming in of healing miracles taking place in each of those places.

Because of all this interest, we were led to form an organization called The International Association of Healing Rooms. The purpose of this new organization is to provide a connection for the Healing Rooms ministries in each city and to provide the tools needed to equip the people who will operate these new Healing Rooms.

So many groups expressed a desire to do their training right in the Healing Rooms in Spokane that we began doing a bimonthly training program to accommodate teams that would be sent from other cities. One brother went home from one of these training programs and raised the dead.

Just as we were preparing to conduct a conference in Knoxville, Tennessee, for the opening of the Healing Rooms there, a team of eight men and women arrived in Spokane from Vancouver, B.C., Canada, to monitor the Healing Rooms and go through the rest of the orientation program. We poured into them and anointed and prayed for them to have the healing ministry.

They were still in Spokane when we left for Knoxville. When we got back home, they had already returned to their homes, but there was a call from one of the men on my answering machine. When he had returned home, he called to his wife, and she didn't respond. He found her lifeless body upstairs in bed. She was cold and gray. She had died in his absence.

In that moment, a holy boldness came over him. He had not spent many days in Spokane in the presence of the Lord for nothing. He could not accept that he had gone off to learn how to bring healing to others, and his own wife had died before he could get back home. He rebuked the spirit of death and called forth life. She gasped, her body jerked, and her spirit came back into her body. He then called the local emergency service, and his wife was transported to the hospital.

His wife is now home. She is off all medications, and she is doing wonderfully.

I had two important visions regarding the healing ministry of the end time, and I see their fulfillment in the extension of the Healing Rooms ministry to other cities. The first vision came to me as I was traveling toward Spokane that very first time. I saw a giant lying in the valley. His head was in Spokane, and his feet extended all the way to Coeur d'Alene, Idaho, thirty miles away. The scene reminded me of the famous Gulliver.

I saw what looked like cobwebs covering the giant — they were threads of some sort. The way they were woven back and forth around him made it look as if he had never moved from his place, as if he had been laid there as a baby and had grown to maturity in that bound condition.

But, in reality, these threads were nothing to such a great giant. He could have moved, but he didn't because he didn't think he could. If he had moved the parts of his body in unison, there was no way those flimsy cords could have held him. He just didn't know that fact.

I sensed that the giant I was seeing was the Church, not just in Spokane, but around the country. If we could just get all of the parts moving together, nothing could hold us back.

I saw the giant begin to stir himself and to move one part and then another, and the cords easily broke off. I saw him free himself entirely and then get up. I sensed that God was about to do something wonderful in His Church in America.

The second vision came to me just before the Healing Rooms were opened. I was driving across the Maple Street Bridge in downtown Spokane before daylight one morning on my way to work in Idaho. As I looked out over the city, I saw that it was darkened. God showed me that the enemy had held God's people captive too long, and the absence of their influence had left darkness to cover the city.

Then I began to see flashes of light, and I wondered where they were coming from. In the Spirit, I was suddenly raised up to the height of the mountains around Spokane, and I could see for great distances. Amazingly, as far as I could see on the outskirts of the city, there were white horses in every direction. On each of those horses sat one of God's warriors, and each warrior held a sword in his hand. It was from the tips of their swords that the flashes of light, almost like lightning, were coming forth.

Then, as I watched, that mighty army began to move in unison. I saw the horses carry the throng to the crest of the hills and then over, and they began to descend into the city. The pounding of hoofs was so powerful that it was shaking the ground in Spokane, and I could see enemies within the city trembling with fear.

As the army descended upon the city, I continued to see lightning flashing from the swords, until it lit up the whole sky over the city. Then something else amazing happened. Suddenly, the windows of Heaven began to open, the sky rolled back, and I was looking into the heavens. A voice like a roaring lion came from Heaven, saying, "Let My people go!"

These visions confirmed the prophecy of Bob Jones, that a healing anointing would begin outside the city of Spokane, come into the city, and then go out from there around the world.

Recently, Bobby Conner came to visit us in the Healing Rooms. He gave me a book that Bob Jones and Keith Davis had put together. On the cover was a painting of Jesus coming on a white horse. His eyes were on fire, and He was holding the sword of the Spirit in His hand. He was coming as the victorious leader of the army I had seen in my vision.

Just down the street a little from the Healing Rooms, the owners of an apartment had a mural painted on the side of their building. It is said to be one of the best exposures for a billboard for cars passing on the freeway. The painting is twenty feet high and thirty-five feet long, and it is that same image of Jesus coming on the white horse. His eyes are on fire, and He has the sword of the Spirit in His hand. From it, lightning flashes forth. The mural is named "King of Glory."

This billboard proclaims the fact that the army of God is rising and will descend on this city and on the nation to bring about the great outpouring God has preordained for this time for the nation and for the world. The greatest move of the Holy Spirit the world has ever seen is about to take place through the Church, through the army that God is calling together and raising up.

Sixteen

The Financing of the Healing Rooms

I must say a word about the financing of the Healing Rooms, as this has often been a point of stumbling for many ministries. As time drew near to re-open the Rooms, this became one of the burdens of my heart. I did not want to spend time worrying about how to pay the rent and continue the work, and I was asking God to do a miracle.

What He showed me was something very simple. I went to the cupboard and found a small Quaker Oats container. There were some oats still in it, so I emptied them into something else. Then I wrapped the small container with a piece of plain white paper. I wrote on it HEALING ROOMS SEED, and I set it in the reception area once we had opened.

Early on, we determined that no charge would be made for those coming to the Healing Rooms for prayer. We would have to trust God to speak to the hearts of His people, and He did.

Later, the Healing Rooms would develop some other sources of income, particularly the sale of our tapes, but that small Quaker Oats container continued to be the major source of our financial supply, and the ministry has grown and prospered since its inception.

After a time, it became apparent that I could not continue my work with the State of Idaho. There was too much demanding my attention in the Healing Rooms. Besides the daily prayer, we had our twice monthly training program for those coming from other cities and countries and our twice monthly conferences in other cities. I needed to be full time in the Healing Rooms ministry.

I sought God about this move because Michelle and I did not want to become a financial burden to this ministry. God showed us that we could have our needs met through the outside conferences, and that is what we have done ever since.

As the ministry of the Healing Rooms has grown, so has God's provision for this ministry.

Now, aside from the many who are coming for prayer, we have extended our ministry to those who cannot come. Several ladies on our team spend time cutting out small prayer cloths to be anointed and sent out all over the world free of charge. They use up to four bolts of cloth each month preparing these prayer cloths. The prayer cloths are stacked up in the prayer room every morning, and our team prays over them. Then, after they have been anointed and prayed over, the cloths are mailed out in response to requests that come in from around the globe.

The same thing is done with our anointing oil.

We have developed a unique oil of our own. In it, we use almond oil (rather than the more commonly used olive oil). With the almond oil, we mix frankincense, myrrh and cinnamon. Our staff makes up thousands of tiny bottles of this oil, and these are sent out free of charge to those who wish to anoint the sick.

We even tell people that if they have been blessed by our tapes, they may freely duplicate them and give them to others.

In this way, our burden, the ministry that the Lord has committed to us, to see as many sick people healed as possible, is accomplished. This brings glory to our Lord Jesus and reveals His love for us, and He responds by providing for our needs in order to accomplish it.

After we began the conferences, enough came in through the Quaker Oats container to buy a fifteen-passenger van and trailer to carry our team, our equipment and our tapes and books. How great the Lord is!

Seventeen

Healing in the Atonement

Some people may wonder how we can be so sure of God's will concerning physical healing, and how we can have such consistent results with those to whom we minister. It is because we believe what God says about healing, just as we believe what He says about salvation.

I have pondered long and hard what it is that has caused the Church of the twenty-first century to be so far from the healing message of the Bible. Our pews are sometimes filled with people who are just as sick as the people of the world. I have come to the conclusion that we do not have an understanding of healing as part of the atonement.

The prophet Isaiah foretold:

Surely our griefs He Himself bore,
And our sorrows He carried;
Yet we ourselves esteemed Him stricken,
Smitten of God, and afflicted.
But He was pierced through for our transgressions,
He was crushed for our iniquities;
The chastening for our well-being fell upon Him,
And by His scourging we are healed.

Isaiah 53:4-5

Jesus carried our sins, our sicknesses and our pains on the cross. Isaiah went on to say:

> *The LORD has caused the iniquity of us all*
> *To fall on Him.*   Isaiah 53:6

Many of us have received an understanding of salvation as part of the atonement, but few seem to have understood that healing is just as much a part of the atonement as is salvation. If we can believe God for salvation through the atonement, on the basis of the promise of Isaiah 53:6, why is it that we can't believe for healing on the basis of Isaiah 53:4?

Many of us have faith for salvation, and when we pray with sinners and lead them in a sinner's prayer, we then say to them, "You are saved." And we believe it.

But how do we know that they are saved? What gives us that assurance? The answer, of course, is that the Word of God promised that it would be so, that if men and women call on God, they will be saved. It's that simple.

But when we pray for sick people, we usually don't give them any such assurance. We tell them we hope they get better, and we then establish the fact that they are healed or not healed based on what we see developing in their conditions in the days after our prayers. A more proper way would be to say what the Word of God says about them, just as we do with salvation.

We receive faith for salvation by hearing the Word of God, and it is the same with healing. There are many promises in God's Word for healing, and we must get them into our spirits, just as we have His promises for salvation.

We pray for sick people, and then we wait and observe to determine whether or not they are healed. If we did that with sinners, it would be quite some time before we could declare that they are genuinely saved. Why do we treat one part of the atonement differently than another?

We must begin to apply the same faith to healing that we do to salvation. We have no right to separate them and treat them differently. By His stripes we are healed, and that is not determined by what we see or how we feel.

A percentage of those for whom we pray in the Healing Rooms are not healed before our eyes, but as they go — just as happened with the lepers in Jesus' day (see Luke 17:14). We could have told Korey Mosher that we were sorry she had not been healed in the Healing Rooms, but we knew better than to do that. Nothing seemed to have changed, but we knew it had, and we acknowledged that fact.

She didn't look any different, but we knew that she was different. Isaiah said so, and so did Jesus. Her healing was part of the atonement, and we accepted that fact, just as much as we did her salvation.

Elaine Mason, a dear lady from Virginia, came to the Healing Rooms. She had developed a cancer on her nose that was affecting the blood vessels around it. Her upper lip was also affected and remained constantly swollen. She had been told that she needed surgery to remove part of her nose and lip. I estimated that Elaine was a woman in her mid-forties, and I could only imagine how this news affected her. Our hearts went out to her the first time we met her.

The Healing Rooms team ministered to Elaine for four days, morning and afternoon. By Saturday of that week, she did not appear to be any better. As she was leaving, however, we told her that she would be healed as she went.

We had poured the promises of the Word of God into Elaine's heart, and we felt that her faith had risen sufficiently that she would be able to lay hold of those provisions as part of her atonement. Sure enough, while Elaine was on the plane headed home, the swelling began to subside and the purple color began to lighten. By the time she got to the next service at her church, her lip and nose were returned nearly to normal. There was still a bit of redness, but her friends could see that God was working and they repented of not having believed.

Elaine's healing had a great impact on her town.

She received it because she believed what Jesus said.

Before any of us can receive a lasting healing for our bodies, we must rid ourselves of all uncertainties concerning God's will to heal today, and God's will to heal *us*. Faith and doubt don't mix. The one is the enemy of the other.

The psalmist declared:

> *I shall not die, but live,*
> *And tell of the works of the LORD.*
>
> Psalm 118:17

How could he be so bold about his healing? Because the Bible makes it very clear that God does not will for us to be sick or to die prematurely. If all of His soldiers are dying, how can He raise up an army? If we are to be mighty warriors, how can we do that from our crutches? If God has called us to go to all the world and preach the Gospel, how can we do that if we are flat on our backs in pain?

It is the enemy who brings poverty upon us. It is the enemy who afflicts us with sickness so that we cannot fulfill our true potential. God sets us free.

Again the psalmist declared:

> *He sent His word and healed them,*
> *And delivered them from their destructions.*
>
> Psalm 107:20

The apostle John taught the same thing, that Jesus had come to *"destroy the works of the devil"*:

> *The Son of God appeared for this purpose, that He might destroy the works of the devil.*
>
> 1 John 3:8

This work did not end when Jesus went back to Heaven. He commanded us to carry on this work. We are to lay hands on the sick and see them healed.

It is time to put healing back in the atonement where it belongs. Why should we settle for half an atonement? Why should we settle for salvation only, when God wants to give us so much more?

The psalmist spoke of the blessings of the atonement:

> *Bless the LORD, O my soul,*
> *And forget none of His benefits;*
> *Who pardons all your iniquities;*
> *Who heals all your diseases;*
> *Who redeems your life from the pit;*
> *Who crowns you with lovingkindness and compassion;*
> *Who satisfies your years with good things,*
> *So that your youth is renewed like the eagle.*
>
> Psalm 103:2-5

These are *"His benefits."* Does God still *"pardon all your iniquities"*? Of course He does. And because of that we know that He also *"heals all your diseases."* We cannot accept the one and reject the other. God has not changed.

As Jesus taught us, truth has a way of setting a person free (see John 8:32). It is time for the Church of Jesus Christ to be steeped in the truths of His healing power, and time for healing to be recognized again as part of the atonement.

— Eighteen —

THE HEALING SEED

How can we have faith for healing? As we know, faith comes by hearing the Word of God, and that Word is described in the Bible as a seed that can grow and bring forth fruit. When we insist on accepting or rejecting our healing on the basis of what we see, we are missing God's best. His Word in us can grow and produce something that is not yet visible.

The Church will never reap a harvest of healing until we get some more good seed sown, just as no farmer expects to reap a harvest without first sowing the seed that will produce it. If the seed is still sitting in the barn, forget about a harvest. It will never come.

I grew up in the country, and when I was still quite young, the thought came to me to plant the seed of a delicious peach I was eating, and then we could have more peaches. My mom told me I had to leave the seed on the drainboard and let it dry out first. I thought that sounded strange, but I did what she said. Then I forgot it.

Later that summer I passed by that seed one day and realized that I had forgotten all about it. I picked it up, only to find that it looked like it was dead.

That was disappointing. Now, how could I grow my peach tree?

Mama told me to go ahead and plant the seed anyway, so I did. Then she told me to go out regularly and water that spot and pull the weeds out of it ... until one day a plant popped through the ground. Sure enough, that peach seed had taken root and grown. That was an exciting experience for a boy, and I never forgot it.

From the beginning, there was life in that seed. The potential was there. But if I had not planted the seed and watered it and weeded it, no plant would ever have come forth. And that wouldn't have been God's fault. It would have been my fault.

If I had left that seed on the drainboard, even for another year, the potential would have been in it, but I would not have had any fruit from it. I released the power of the seed when I planted it, and that is exactly what we must do with God's Word.

The potential for increase is inherent in the seed of the Word of God, but it is what we do with that seed that determines whether or not we will have a harvest from it. For instance, I couldn't go out a week after I had first planted that seed and dig it up to see if it was growing. I had to leave it in the ground.

That potential for increase that is in the seed of God's Word is *"the substance of things hoped for."* We release that substance by doing what God requires. When we get the seed of His Word (*"by*

His stripes we are healed") into our hearts, and we hold fast to it, and nurture it and walk in it, that seed will surely begin to produce a harvest. This happens when we refuse to walk by what we see, but by what God says.

When seeds are properly sown, there will be a harvest. But from the time the seed is planted until you begin to see the harvest coming forth, you must walk by faith. You can't see the seed growing until the plant pops through the ground and becomes evident for all to see. A good farmer, however, knows what is happening under the earth.

Once you are healed, faith is no longer required. Anyone can see the result. By faith, you can know it long before it becomes apparent to others. Faith operates in the unseen realm and brings forth something that can then be seen. We must come to expect the natural world to line up with the spiritual world, not the other way around. The seed is not determined by the harvest; it is the harvest that is determined by the seed.

What we cannot see is more real than what we can see. The created must obey the Creator. Through God's Word, we can bring about a reordering of things, and healing then becomes a sign to unbelievers that God is real.

Our faith for healing must be based on nothing other than God's Word. It certainly cannot come from the things we see or hear or feel around us.

Faith that is not acted upon can become dead faith. Faith, when we act upon it, is powerful and produces results:

> *"Therefore I say to you, all things for which you pray and ask, believe that you have received them, and they shall be granted you."*   Mark 11:24

"All things!" Now that's powerful.

But how do we receive them? Jesus was saying that we must count it as done. *"Believe that you have received them."* This is the way in which we release the power of the Word to produce after itself.

We are not told to believe after we receive the healing we seek, but to believe at the time we receive the seed for it. Plant the seed, so that you can have the harvest of healing it will produce. This is an important key to greater miracles of healing.

John wrote to the first-century Church:

> *And this is the confidence which we have before Him, that, if we ask anything according to His will, He hears us. And if we know that He hears us in whatever we ask, we know that we have the requests which we have asked from Him.*
>
> 1 John 5:14-15

"We know that we have" ... even before we see the results. That's faith.

Can it fail? No. God's Word will always produce what He has sent it to produce. He has assured us that it will never return void to Him. Our faith, therefore, must not be based on what happens in the natural realm but upon what God has said.

Don't wait for the healing to begin before you begin to believe. That is the opposite of what God has said. Don't wait until part of your healing comes to believe for the rest. Let the same seed that brings part of your healing bring forth a full healing.

Many people lose their healing because they turn their attention from the seed of God's promise and concentrate on their circumstances or symptoms. Pain, for instance, is a terrible distraction.

This is the reason that in the Healing Rooms we give the people who come the Word of God. We attempt to establish the healing scriptures in their hearts. For instance, we supply each sick person who has been ministered to a printed sheet with guidelines on how to keep your healing. This is important, because we know that the enemy will try to use symptoms to discourage the people and make them believe they have not been healed.

This should not come as a surprise to any of us. It was the enemy who brought the infirmity in the first place, and he doesn't like it when we begin to receive the manifestation of our healing. He wants to steal God's glory that has brought forth that healing. When symptoms begin to return, we must recognize them for what they are — lies of the devil.

When the symptoms of your sickness begin to return, that is the moment in which it will become apparent what you will do with God's promise. You can either cast it aside and believe Satan's lies, or you can cling to God's Word and reject the enemy's attempts to deceive you.

If you have been healed of a foot condition, the enemy delights in putting a pain back into that foot, just to see what you will do. Jesus described this work of the wicked one.

> *"And those beside the road are those who have heard; then the devil comes and takes away the word from their heart, so that they may not believe and be saved."* Luke 8:12

And, of course, the same is true of the healing seed. He will attempt to snatch it away from you immediately. When it happens, it is your choice. Will you believe the symptom? Or will you believe God's Word? You can break that attack when it comes by refusing delivery.

If someone were to send you a special delivery package full of hissing rattlesnakes, would you accept delivery of it? Or would you mark it "return to sender" and let it go back where it came from? It's your choice. You don't have to accept what the devil wants to deliver to you. Cling to the Word of

God, no matter what you feel and no matter what you see.

Keith Gutenberger, a Presbyterian teenager, had suffered from migraine headaches for four years. The headaches were so severe that the drugs required to make the pain bearable put him out of commission. He was no longer able to continue his schooling, and he had lost hope of going on to college, marrying and living a normal life.

Keith's mom called me one day. She was the secretary for their church, and Keith's dad was the choir director. They had heard about the Healing Rooms and wanted to know if I thought we could help Keith.

"In the past four years," she told me that day, "we have taken Keith to every kind of prayer service imaginable. Why should I believe that this will be any different?"

"You've been seeking healing all this time?" I asked.

"We have," she assured me.

"Well, what you need now," I told her, "is just to get into the presence of the Lord. Get face-to-face with the Healer, and Keith will be healed." They decided to give us a try.

They brought Keith to the Healing Rooms one day not long after that, a team prayed for him, and his migraines disappeared. The mom and dad were absolutely ecstatic. They were prayed for too, and they fell under the power of God and lay on the floor, full of the Spirit and blessed.

Just a week later, Keith's symptoms returned, and his mom called to ask what they should do. "Bring him down," I told her. This time we explained to them about the lying nature of Satan and his attempts to deceive us all. We laid hands on Keith once more, and the migraines left and never returned.

Keith was able to join other young people from his church on a mission trip to Mexico, and he was able to go to college. After that, we had a steady stream of Presbyterians coming to the Healing Rooms because Keith and his parents had testified in their church about what God had done for him.

Since healing is a finished work, the Lord desires that our healing be a permanent thing. Our healing, therefore, does not depend on how we feel, but upon what He has done.

We must declare, *"By His stripes I am healed."* We may not yet be able to see the result, but it is a reality, nevertheless. We must receive the Word of the Lord concerning our healing, and then we must walk in that word. The writer of Hebrews gave us a guide for doing this. He said:

Therefore, do not throw away your confidence, which has a great reward. For you have need of endurance, so that when you have done the will of God, you may receive what was promised.

Hebrews 10:35-36

This is where many people fail to receive their healing. God is telling us not to *"throw away"* our confidence because a seed always produces a harvest. It may reside as yet in the unseen realm, but we can trust what God has said.

To receive healing, we often *"have need of endurance."* This endurance speaks of consistency and constancy. Be steadfast with what God has given you and you will receive the intended benefit. What good is the Word if it is not given an opportunity to produce something in you? What good is a seed if it cannot produce a harvest? God wants to give us more than just seed. His will is to give us the harvest that seed is capable of producing.

Nineteen

Our Solid Foundation

Our faith rests on far more solid ground than the sometimes contrary evidence perceived by our natural senses. This faith rests on the unchanging Word of God that will abide forever, and it is a creative force in us.

The Bible says that *"faith is the substance of things hoped for"* (Hebrews 11:1, KJV). So it is not what you hope for; it is the substance of what you hope for. There is a creative power in that seed, and it can be released — depending on what you do with the seed.

Our faith does not depend on how we feel, because it is more real than our sickness. If the Word of God created the world and everything in it, then doesn't it make sense that the world and everything in it is subject to the Creator?

If Jesus came to destroy the work of the devil, and the infirmity that is in us is the work of the devil, then that work needs to be destroyed. That is a message for Christians. We would not allow the lost to come into our church services and become involved in our programs and think nothing of it. We would have a burden to get them saved. Still, we allow sick people to be involved in our churches at every level, and we think nothing of it. Why let them suffer? It is time to prevail against sickness. Jesus came to destroy it, just as He came to destroy our sin.

When people get sick, the first thing they do is call a doctor, and most Christians are no different. Why is it that we don't think first of going to Doctor Jesus? In the Healing Rooms we don't tell people *not* to go to the doctor, but we expect the day to come when they will be built up in their faith and no longer need the help of doctors.

The fact that we go to the doctor in the natural cannot be allowed to determine what our faith for healing is. Our faith for healing does not come through a doctor. It comes through the Word of God. If you are being attended to by a medical doctor, and you receive divine healing, often that doctor will love you for it. His work is finished.

We must begin to move from having a dependency on the natural world to having a dependency on the spiritual world. After all, the spiritual world is more real because it created the natural. This dependency on the spiritual world will cause us to be moved, not by what we see, but by what we hear from God. That will change what we see.

When we become convinced, through God's Word, that our prayers are answered — before we have seen those answers — then we can know that the Word is effectually working in us. This releases the creative power, the force of faith, to begin to produce in us. Faith rejoices in the promises of God, as if the problems were already resolved and we are now enjoying it.

Occasionally, we see an individual or couple on the news who has won the lottery. They are holding their winning ticket up for everyone to see, and it is obvious that they are very happy. They are already making plans about how they will spend the money they have won.

The truth is that they have no money. All they have is a ticket. If they had read the numbers wrong on that ticket, even if they were mistaken by only one digit, they would lose their expected winnings. But right now, they are not worried about anything like that. They are excited and rejoicing because they are sure they have the winning number. They are sure their flimsy paper ticket will be exchanged for the winning prize.

Why can't we Christians have that kind of faith? Why is it that we have more confidence in a lottery ticket than we do in the Word of God? Which is greater? The odds of winning the lottery are staggering, but the promises of the Word of God never fail.

God's Word always produces what it was sent to produce. Get your gear shifted from a natural dependency to a supernatural dependency, and you will begin to see all that God has promised you.

Don't doubt your faith. Doubt your doubts. Faith is something, while doubt is nothing.

We must begin to believe like Jesus believed. We must follow His example. He said, *"They shall recover."* We need to begin to take that same stand. You can tell the enemy, "It is written; I will recover."

If it is wrong, as some say, to declare that we know God will heal us, then it is also wrong for the farmer to expect a harvest when he plants his crop. We not only declare, as many do, that God is able. We also declare that He is willing and in fact that the work has been accomplished.

It is not enough to *hope* for healing. Too many people say, "Well, I hope I'm healed." Hope is somewhere in the possibility of the future, while faith is a present reality. We can't hope it will happen; we must know so. When you develop a "know-so" faith, God will work for you.

Many are still doubting whether or not God actually wants to heal us. Believe me, He wants to do it far more than we want to receive it. If God sent Jesus to die on the cross to give us this provision, that's a pretty good indication to me of what He wants to do.

Twenty

Rise Up, Church

Most of those who come to the Healing Rooms are churched people. We are glad for them to come and be healed, but if the churches were doing their work, there would not be so many sick Christians.

Just as God meant our salvation experience to be permanent and for us to walk in it every day, His healing for our bodies was also meant to be permanent. He wants us to be healed and to live in health. That is His provision for us.

Just as God has not called us to walk in depression and marital turmoil, he has also not called us to walk in sickness. If we are to be an army, we must be raised up individually to serve. Each of us must receive what we personally need to live victoriously so that we can be able to minister to others. God's army cannot be constantly held back by enemy forces. If we never get out of our tents, how can we do the great work God is calling us to?

God's army must be filled with His power and must walk in His presence. Some of us have the helmet of salvation cocked over to one side, the breastplate of righteousness on upside down, and the sword of the Spirit stuck to our feet. God wants us to begin to get this right. Then we will be able to march forth as a mighty army, and to take back what the devil has stolen from us. That's our commission.

In the Healing Rooms, our vision goes beyond Spokane, Washington, and beyond the Healing Rooms being established in other cities. God wants to raise up an army and has burdened us for the Church worldwide. The great harvest is ready. Rise up, Church. This is the day of great revival.

Healing will be like an undergarment for God's warriors to wear. Our armor will rest upon it. If soldiers are sick, they must be taken out of battle. That's serious today because we have so many sick that few are left to battle. God wants your sickness to be overcome.

It is time to move out of our tents and to take our places on the front lines. When the enemy looks at our ranks, he must not see a dispirited and exhausted band. Let him see a mighty army and flee in terror.

We must rise up in power to resist the devil with great force, walking in signs and wonders. Arise, to take the spoil and to reap the great end-time harvest.

Jesus, our Bridegroom, is anxious to come back, but when He does, He will be looking for a prepared Bride. This is what our current signs and wonders movement is all about. It is preparing the Church and it is enabling us to reap the harvest of souls.

The prophets, whom God has placed in the Church, are not speaking less healing, but more healing. They are not speaking of diminishing healing power for the Church, but an increasing anointing in this regard.

The devil has had his way far too long. It's our turn. Rise up, Church. As the world has been possessed of the devil, let us now be possessed of God, possessed of His power, possessed of His love. Let us be so possessed that it will be evident to people everywhere we go.

God wants His Church to be visible in the world around us, for He wants to demonstrate His love and power everywhere. It is time that men are moved to tears just by standing near us in a checkout line and feeling God's presence that accompanies us.

One day two ladies came into the Healing Rooms in Spokane off the street, seemingly by accident. They were provocatively dressed, and one of them was covered with tattoos. They had been looking for a county aid office that was formerly located in that building, but was no longer there.

Next to the elevator they saw a sign that read: HEALING ROOMS, THIRD FLOOR. They couldn't imagine what this might mean, so they decided to go up and see. When they got out of the elevator on the third floor and the doors closed behind them, they had the strange feeling that they were somehow trapped.

The worship music from the reception area was drifting out into the corridor, and they were strangely moved by it. Suddenly, they both felt very lost. Until that moment, they hadn't known how very lost they were.

Tears were already streaming down the faces of the two ladies when Cyndy, our receptionist, saw them. She went over and took them by the arm, saying, "We want to pray for you."

One of the ladies said, "But we have no money."

"Honey, it's free," she assured them.

It seemed difficult for them to believe that something so wonderful could be free.

The two ladies were escorted into the Silver Room, where they were prayed over, and that day they met Jesus face-to-face. I'll never forget seeing the lady with the tattoos as she was on her way out that day. As she passed a painting in the reception area of Jesus with His arms outstretched, she turned and looked at Him. Then she kissed her fingers and reached over and touched Him with them. As she did so, I heard her say, "Thank You."

It's all about God's presence.

Have you ever been lost in the woods? It's not so bad until you suddenly realize you are lost, and then a terrible desperation comes over you. I am seeing that same kind of desperation in the world today. Men are lost and they know they are lost, and they suddenly want very much to be found. This is a wonderful time for Christians to be living.

God wants to heal us so that we can turn and heal our cities and our nations. Rise up, Church. Be healed, and go forth to heal and save.

Instead of arriving at church seeking only to meet a few of our own personal needs, it is time that we come expecting to be equipped to go out and minister to the world around us. Sunday worship is wonderful and necessary, but this time with God must prepare us for what we will face on Monday and the rest of the week.

It is time for the Church to get out of the four walls of our sanctuaries and begin to do the work of the Lord. He has commissioned us to go into the enemy's camp and take back what has been stolen from us. God wants to move in WalMart, in city hall, in the classrooms of our schools and in our places of business. His work is where people are to be found, and often that is not in church. We can no longer expect everyone to come to us. We must go to them, and when we do, they must see the power of God at work in our lives.

Let the Word of God dwell richly in your own life, and then let it bring healing to all those around you who are suffering. It is time to learn, not only how to receive what God has promised for our own lives, but also how to impart it to others.

Rise up, Church.

In Jesus' name.
Amen!

AFTERWORD

As of this writing, some three hundred and fifty people each week from all over the U.S. and from other countries are being ministered to in the Healing Rooms, two healing conferences are being conducted each month in other cities around America, and Healing Rooms are being opened in many other cities across this country and around the world. We are continually seeking God for an increased anointing for healing.

What a wonderful day to be alive! The God of John G. Lake is at work in the twenty-first century.

John Lake was one of sixteen children, and as he was growing up, he saw eight of his siblings die of one disease or another. This left a deep impression on him. Later in life, he would write that for thirty-two years there had always been an invalid in his family, and "during this period, our home was never without the shadow of sickness. As I think back over my boyhood and young manhood, there comes to mind remembrances like a nightmare — sickness, doctors, nurses, hospitals, hearses, funerals, graveyards, tombstones, a sorrowing household, a brokenhearted mother and a grief-stricken father struggling to forget the sorrows of the past in order to assist the living members of the family who needed their love and care." [1] It was perhaps as a result of this tragic family experience that throughout his life, John G. Lake hated sickness with a passion. This deep-rooted hatred of disease surely must have contributed to the development of the wonderful healing power that came upon his life.

At one point, he nearly lost his own wife. She was seriously ill and nearly died. It was during that time of severe stress that he received a great revelation about God's power. Frustrated and not understanding what was happening, he set his Bible down and it opened to Acts 10:38, and there he read: *"how God anointed Jesus of Nazareth with the Holy Ghost and with power: who went about doing good, and healing all that were oppressed of the devil; for God was with him."* In that moment, John G. Lake understood that Jesus is the Healer and Satan the oppressor, and he became convinced that God's will was to heal all sick people everywhere.

This vision led him to found the Healing Rooms in Spokane, Washington, and it was a similar vision that led us to reopen them again eighty years later. We thank God for anointed men like John G. Lake who were forerunners of this revival. But we thank God, most of all, that He hasn't changed. He is the same:

Jesus Christ is the same yesterday and today, yes and forever. Hebrews 13:8

This truth is confirmed by the healing miracles the Lord is performing in the reopened Healing Rooms in Spokane, and wherever men or women of faith will allow Him to work in their lives.

In closing, I want to share with you one more testimony of God's great healing power: Just recently, a lady named Linda Davies came to the Healing Rooms. Linda was raised in Spokane, where her family still resides. In her young adulthood, she moved to Fort Worth, Texas, and spent twenty-five of her forty-one years bound to drugs and alcohol.

In the fall of 2000, her health was declining rapidly, and she learned that she was HIV-positive. Her doctor suggested that she return to Spokane to spend the rest of her days with her family.

Through all of this, Linda accepted Jesus as her Savior and was delivered from drugs and alcohol. Then she heard about the Healing Rooms and began to come for prayer. She came every Thursday for five months.

When she started coming to us, Linda had (as she states it) thirty-five thousand parts of HIV in her blood. After five months she was feeling so good that she went to her doctor and asked to be tested. She was convinced that God had healed her. To the doctor's amazement, the HIV was no longer at any detectable level in her bloodstream. Praise God!

Linda has now gone through our training and is ministering to others what God has done for her.

I thank the Lord that He has taken away my life and given me His. What a joy it is to realize that Linda and others like her are worth every sacrifice.

1. *John G Lake: His Life, His Sermons, His Boldness of Faith* (Fort Worth, Texas: Kenneth Copeland Publications, 1994) page 237.

Ministry address:

Cal Pierce
Healing Rooms Ministries
112 East First Avenue
Spokane, Washington 99202
(509) 456-0517
www.healingrooms.com